Beyond
Ever After

Beyond
Ever After

A Heart-to-Heart Journey
Through Death and the Afterlife

CATHERINE A. WEISSENBERG
JOCELYN MONTANARO

Beyond
Ever After
PRESS

Beyond Ever After Press
P.O. Box 3496, Santa Barbara, CA 93130
www.beyondeverafter.com

ISBN: 978-1-7331727-3-8 (softcover)
ISBN: 978-1-7331727-5-2 (hardcover)
ISBN: 978-1-7331727-2-1 (ebook)

Library of Congress Control Number: 2019909271

Cover Design by Damonza
Interior Design by Sun Editing & Book Design

Printed in the United States of America
First printing edition 2019

This book is based on Jocelyn Montanaro's experiences during her late husband's illness and describes some of the medical issues and decisions that arose in his treatment. However, this book is not intended to give medical information or advice, and the reader is encouraged to consult an appropriate professional on all health issues. The information contained in this book is intended to be inspirational and not for diagnosis, prescription, or treatment of any health or psychological disorder whatsoever. Neither the publisher nor the authors have engaged in rendering professional advice or services to the individual reader. The ideas, procedures, and suggestions contained in this book are not intended to substitute for consulting with your physician, psychologist or other healthcare provider on all matters of concern, including suicidal thoughts out of longing to be reunited with a loved one who has passed away. All matters regarding your health require medical supervision. Neither the authors nor the publisher shall be liable for any loss or damage allegedly arising from the information or suggestions in this book. The information should not replace consultation with a competent healthcare or mental health professional. The authors and publisher are in no way liable for any misuse of the material contained in this book.

For the one I love, my husband and partner in all things.

—C.W.

To my beautiful and talented sister Victoria Garske, whose wise counsel and uncharacteristic prodding led me to begin this journey with Catherine and Kevin. Love you, Vic!

And to my husband Kevin, the love of my life, the heart of my soul.

—J.M.

CONTENTS

FOREWORD

Gary E. Schwartz, PhD

I have a unique gift, which I didn't ask for,
and don't know why it was given to me....
*It is literally an **unlimited calling card** to connect with God,*
and it was given to me 30 years ago.
I don't mean to boast by calling it a gift;
it's just the best way to describe it....
While the majority of the work I do with people
is facilitating a God energy connection for them,
I also make contact with the hereafter.

— *Catherine A. Weissenberg*

I pay attention to synchronicities—meaningful coincidences that connect people with each other and with a greater reality. You can imagine my feelings of surprise and gratitude when I coincidentally read the above sentences (the words *"unlimited calling card"* were bolded by me) two days after I

Gary E. Schwartz, PhD, is Professor of Psychology, Medicine, Neurology, Psychiatry, and Surgery, and Director of the Laboratory for Advances in Consciousness and Health, at the University of Arizona. He has written eight books for the general public, including *The Afterlife Experiments, The G.O.D. Experiments, Super Synchronicity,* and *Greater Reality Living* (with Dr. Mark Pitstick).

i

had seemingly spontaneously written the sentence *Changing the World, One **Call** at a Time,* as the new subtitle for my next book titled *The SoulPhone Revolution.* The SoulPhone involves the use of emerging technology for the purpose of communicating with people in the hereafter. The "unlimited calling card" / "one call at a time" synchronicity is a gracious reminder of the precious nature of *Beyond Ever After* and its messages of hope, inspiration, and love.

Being an academic scientist, my responsibility is to question everything, to keep an open mind and heart as I seek evidence, and to follow the findings where they take me. When someone like Catherine claims that she receives communication not only from those who have physically died, but also from the God energy itself, my first responsibility is to remain agnostic and ask the question, "Where is the evidence?"

I should explain that I agreed to write this Foreword not only because of the book's important practical as well as spiritual information and messages, but because the authors of the book provide enough compelling evidence to justify sharing their remarkable journey of illness and love, pain and humor with their readers. In addition, I requested two "God writings" with Catherine and received striking personal confirmatory evidence.

Consider the following surprising evidence provided by Jocelyn Montanaro, the co-author of this book:

> JOCELYN [to Kevin]: How are you? I don't care about myself. I only care about you.
>
> KEVIN [Jocelyn's husband in a coma, as perceived and reported by Catherine]: So where does that leave my opinion about how I care about you? She Who Must be Obeyed...
>
> JOCELYN [to Catherine]: He used to call me "she who must be obeyed ..."

This was a joke between us. "She Who Must be Obeyed" was from a movie and was slang for "My Wife Who Must be in Charge." Kevin thought it was really funny and would call me "She Who Must be Obeyed" sometimes and then laugh at his own joke. He really was a goofball in a lot of ways.

Or, consider the following compelling evidence:

KEVIN: No way! Are you joking? I'm dreaming. This is not possible, Joc. What are you saying? I know what you're describing but what is wrong with me?

Up to this point, Kevin hadn't said anything that was really personal to us. I didn't really know Catherine, but my sister Vicky did. Vicky could have told Catherine the names of our kids, but when he called me Joc, which is what Kevin always called me, I started to believe it was really him. There was only one way to find out if it was really Kevin I was talking to.

And this evidence:

JOCELYN: What's the last thing you remember, sweetie?

KEVIN: I remember before going into surgery, reaching up and taking Linda's hand and saying, "Thank you for doing this, Linda."

At this point, I nearly fell off my chair. That was almost verbatim what the surgeon told me Kevin said to her before he went into surgery. I knew, beyond a shadow of a doubt, that I was talking to Kevin. There was no way Catherine could have known this.

FYI, I almost fell off my chair reading this. I again almost fell off my chair after reading their account of an impressive "Experiment" proposed and conducted by Kevin (you'll have to read the book for this).

Of course, the skeptical reader might question whether the co-authors of this book can be trusted to be accurate and/or truthful reporters. There is ultimately no substitute for direct personal experience and verification. I was privileged to have the opportunity to receive such verification. For example, according to Catherine, in response to my explanation that I was at a crossroads in my professional and personal life, and wished to receive possible guidance from the source, Catherine used a metaphor that she attributed to God about shifting my focus from being "behind the horse" to "galloping on the horse" and seeking the "high country." What Catherine did not know, and only my wife and a few of our closest colleagues and friends knew, was that we had just begun actively using the metaphors of "not putting the cart before the horse" and seeking information "directly from the horse's mouth." Moreover, we had recently heard a new wisdom statement, "when you come to a fork in the road, go up," and had decided to adopt it as a guiding principle.

When we consider the compelling evidence reported in *Beyond Ever After,* and then consider the striking evidence from my personal observations of Catherine, we have strong reason to read (and reread) this book with open minds and hearts.

The authors of this book are well-educated and successful professionals. Catherine holds a Master of Arts degree in Communication, Jocelyn has a bachelor's degree in International Studies as well as a law degree (Kevin also had a law degree). Both of the authors are mothers who love their children. Each writes with her own unique voice, and they complement one another beautifully. And enjoyably for the reader, both have a sense of humor. I especially enjoyed reading the following sentences about Jocelyn on their website:

> "That Jocelyn would write a book about accepting God's love and communicating with the dead was about as likely as her being elected Pope. Jack Reacher was her preferred protagonist, not Jesus. Perhaps a display of God's sense of humor and irony, this is Jocelyn's story—a story with herself, Kevin, God and his psychic side-kick as the main characters."

Parenthetically, one of my favorite novelists is Lee Child, and one of my favorite characters is Jack Reacher. I might also confess that I share Jocelyn's and Kevin's appreciation for James Taylor.

As you will see, *Beyond Ever After* provides a "window into unseen realms of mystery, spirit and our connection to a divine, infinite source or creator." Catherine is careful to explain her non-denominational approach when she envisions the source.

> "While I will refer to this all-loving source as 'God,' I don't believe this source is fixed, limited or proprietary in name or expression. Each of us has our own unique personal experience and concepts of this infinite creator and energy (e.g., a Higher Power, Yahweh, Brahman, Buddha, Elohim, the Source, Allah, etc.). In this book, this source is referred as 'God.' If you find the 'God' vocabulary off-putting, you can use a descriptor consistent with your spiritual framework."

I shared the same philosophy in my book *The G.O.D. Experiments: How Science is Discovering God in Everything, Including Us,* where G.O.D. stands for the more scientifically framed concept of a "Guiding-Organizing-Designing" process in the universe.

If you sense that I deeply admire and celebrate this book (and its authors, including Kevin), you are correct. I trust that *Beyond Ever After* will speak to your heart as well as your head, and that it will inspire you to expand your visions of soul, spirit, source, and the greater reality.

—Gary E. Schwartz, PhD

CHAPTER 1

A NICE STATE OF NORMAL

Jocelyn

You know how you go through life and it has its ups and downs, but it's mostly okay? Of course you would always like to have more money, have your kids do better in school and be better behaved at home, keep your house cleaner, and maybe drop a little weight. But in general, you think things are relatively fine.

Until Kevin was diagnosed with brain cancer in 2009, that's how our lives were. He had a successful business as a legal mediator. Our youngest son was nine, our older son 19, both doing relatively well. We were financially stable. After a few years of personal losses such as deaths in the family, things had settled into a nice state of normal.

I had planned a surprise trip to Hawaii for the Christmas break. I didn't even tell Kevin but simply cleared his work calendar. I finally let him know about the surprise a few weeks before we were to leave.

Kevin enjoyed Hawaii. He loved to surf and was excited to bring his board and catch some tropical waves. We spent ten days on Kauai, our favorite island, staying at a resort right by the water. The weather was perfect the entire time and we were having the best vacation we had ever had.

I have a vivid memory of Kevin on our last full day reading his book in a restaurant by the water. Snacking on bar mix and drinking a beer as the Lakers played in the background, he looked at me and said, "Life doesn't get much better than this."

On the morning of our departure, we planned to enjoy one final snorkel before packing up and flying home in the afternoon. But when Kevin woke up, he felt sick to his stomach. Since he rarely had an upset stomach, I attributed it to the fish we ate and the beer we drank the evening before. I was standing on the balcony watching the waves crash as the sun rose.

Despite Kevin not feeling well and not up for snorkeling, we'd had a great trip. While I was sad to be leaving, I had wonderful memories—and a killer tan. Happy and relaxed, I thought of how good life was. "I'm such a lucky woman," I reminisced.

As I was peering out over the water, I heard what sounded like a monkey screeching behind me. I've thought a lot about that moment over the last several years, because that was when our lives changed forever. As I turned in the direction of the noise, one of our kids yelled, "Dad!"

Kevin was standing by the bed, his body rigid and shaking. I ran over to him as he started to fall. Fortunately, we were able to catch him before he hit the floor. I thought he must be having a heart attack. When a 56-year-old man keels over, that's usually the reason. Running to the phone, I dialed 911, remaining on the phone until the emergency services arrived. Even though it was under ten minutes, it felt like a lifetime. Although Kevin had stopped shaking, he was unconscious and didn't seem to be breathing normally. As the paramedics entered the room, his eyes fluttered open, though he was clearly disoriented.

I rode in the ambulance with him, while our kids followed in our rental car. At the hospital Kevin regained full consciousness.

When the doctor asked him if he knew where he was, he responded, "The hospital?"

I related what had happened for the doctor, though by now I realized that Kevin had experienced a seizure. I knew what one looked like since, following a bicycle accident, my older son had undergone a seizure when he was a child.

When the doctor showed me Kevin's MRI, I was shocked to see the clear image of an egg-sized tumor. Stepping out to the waiting room, I told our kids that their father had a brain tumor.

I knew then that our relatively normal life was over.

CHAPTER 2

"WHAT'S THE LAST THING THAT YOU REMEMBER?"

Jocelyn

Modern medicine gave Kevin the gift of an extended life. In 2009, he underwent successful brain surgery to remove the tumor, followed by months of radiation and chemotherapy. Tragically, almost three and a half years after that last day in Hawaii, Kevin's scans revealed that the cancer had returned.

We found ourselves back at UCLA. Given that the first surgery had been so successful, we naively hoped this second one would go off without a hitch. Instead, I found myself staying with Kevin around the clock because he had suffered a cascade of devastating complications only minutes after being wheeled from the operating table into recovery. He was in the Neuro ICU and was comatose for the next 26 days. It was at this point that Catherine came into the picture.

I first heard about Catherine through my sister Vicky. They had been friends for years. Vicky told me about how Catherine could communicate not only with people who had died but also directly with God. Being a skeptic and a lawyer, I thought this was ridiculous. I suspected that Catherine just fed people's need to communicate with their deceased loved ones; that there was no way she could actually do what Vicky described. Honestly, I didn't think too highly of Catherine.

I had met Catherine one evening when we were both substitutes at a Bunko game night. My first impression was that she was nothing like the image I had conjured up of a presumptuous woman wearing flowing colorful clothing, bangles on her wrists, and the scent of incense wafting around her. What a surprise to discover she was just like me—a middle-aged mother who drove a minivan with a few extra pounds around her middle. Far from being presumptuous, she was smart and funny. We clicked instantly. There was no mention of her "gift" that evening, or on the couple of occasions when I ran into her over the next few years.

When Kevin fell into a coma after his surgery, my sister told me that Catherine was willing to do a "writing" for me, a term she used because it was her practice to write down the messages she received. Vicky said the writings captured communications directly from God, and sometimes from people who had died. To do a writing for someone in a coma was nothing unusual for Catherine.

My initial response was that I did not want a writing. Why would I, as pissed off at God as I was for taking Kevin from me? The last thing I was interested in was some religious speak about it being "God's will" or how Kevin was going to a better place. I didn't want my husband to go to a better place; I wanted him here with me. I said no to the writing.

My sister persisted, "If you don't want a writing, Catherine said she'd pray with you." There was no way I was interested in praying with her. Hadn't I been praying like crazy, with Kevin only continuing to deteriorate?

Though I had turned to prayer, as so many of us do in a situation of this kind, the truth was I had never been a religious person. I really hoped there was a God—who doesn't? Heaven sounded great. If there was one, I certainly wanted to go. But I wasn't a believer. Quite the opposite, I'm the type who needs a direct experience before I'm willing to believe something.

Unlike me, many people believed in Catherine and her gift. In the end I relented only because I felt that at this point I had nothing to lose. What if, against all odds, there was some truth to what others were saying about her?

So I set up a time for a phone writing with Catherine. I was staying with Kevin at the UCLA hospital where he was comatose, and Catherine was a thousand miles away.

Soon after Catherine began the writing session, I asked Kevin through her, "What's the last thing that you remember?"

When Catherine relayed Kevin's answer, I was stunned. "Right before getting wheeled into surgery, I remember reaching up to take Linda's hand and saying 'Thank you for doing this Linda'." I nearly dropped the phone because I knew I was truly communicating with Kevin, even though he was in a comatose state.

Catherine had no way of knowing that after the operation, Dr. Linda Liau met with the children and me to report on how the procedure had gone. Before she launched into the details, she relayed the words Kevin had spoken to her before the surgery. It was so like him to have reached up from the gurney to take her hand and tell her, "Thank you for doing this, Linda."

The only people who knew this were our children and me. After Dr. Liau shared it with me, I didn't repeat it to anyone. As Catherine uttered the exact words Dr. Liau had reported, I knew she was for real. Catherine really could communicate with people who were comatose or dead.

That first writing, on August 5, 2013, began the next phase of my relationship with Kevin. We have subsequently engaged in many writings, as a result of which I now know that God exists. I no longer fear dying, because I know that when someone dies, they are not really gone. I know that the essence of who they are continues, including the same sense of humor. They also know what's going on with us, down to uncanny specifics. They feel love even more keenly because it's of a purer form. While they aren't strictly "here," they are not really gone either. I'm certain that when I die, I'm going to be with Kevin again.

My wish is that when you finish reading our story, which is really a love story, you will feel hope. I want you to know that even if you can't communicate with them, the people you love who have gone before you are still with you. Mostly, I want you to know that there is a life after the one we experience here on Earth, so that you don't fear death. As Kevin said in one of the writings, "Death isn't a failure."

I think almost everyone fears death because they don't really know what happens after. But I now know what happens after, and while I hope to live to an old age and see my children have families of their own, I know that when I leave this Earth there is something even better for me on the other side.

CHAPTER 3

A GIFT FROM GOD

Catherine

I didn't ask for the unique gift that's been entrusted to me. All I know is that it comes from God. In truth, all of our lives are a gift from God—and yet my particular gift is different because it's literally an unlimited calling card to connect with God, given to me 30 years ago.

When my friend Vicky asked me to write for Jocelyn, I could never have imagined that it would lead to an ongoing journey of love, loss, reconnection, and spirituality. Nor could I have imagined that you, dear reader, would be sharing this journey and story with us.

While the majority of the work I do with people involves facilitating a divine connection for them, I also make contact with the hereafter. This connection takes a written form that I call "God writings." I don't place calls to the hereafter, nor am I a channel or medium. I prefer to describe my work as dipping into an always-available stream of consciousness and writing down what I find there. Although I'm certainly inspired by what I receive from the divine or the spirit of a deceased person or comatose individual, I'm not merely taking dictation from these sources.

Regardless of whether the energy is from God or an individual, the connection is as vibrant and real as anything I experience on earth. The energy has form and feeling, but not words in the familiar kind of human context. Expansive and full of sensory and energetic experiences, it's a form of connectivity that defies translation.

My process requires more than quieting the mind or meditating. It involves inviting and activating a different form of reception and expansion. This involves not only sensing myself, but also merging with an energy that's simultaneously part of me and yet separate from me. Although my offering is unique, I believe that we all have the capacity to experience this kind of connection. Each of us is intrinsically one with this divine energy.

This is a story about the relationship between a husband and wife. It's also the story of a man and his faith, as well as the relationship of our human attachments to and beliefs about spirituality, the afterlife, and reality itself. It's about the power of connection and a love that even death can't extinguish.

In this story, you are invited into the most intimate and private moments between Kevin and Jocelyn, as their spiritual journeys evolve. You'll also be given a firsthand view and experience of this gift and its power to impact others. As you read, you may be called to explore your own beliefs about love, human potential, and what awaits us when we die. More specifically, your sense of a fixed reality with solid boundaries may be stretched as you are guided to consider a more expansive and fluid sense of expression and connection.

This book provides a window into unseen realms of mystery, spirit, and our connection to an infinite source or creator. As you will learn, Kevin refers to his understanding of our source as God. He happens to see God in terms of Jesus, since he grew up embracing Christianity. I see no reason to believe that this source is fixed, limited, or proprietary in either name or expression. Each of us has our unique personal experience and concept of this infinite creative energy, which is often spoken of as a Higher Power, Yahweh, Brahman, Buddha, Elohim, the Source, Allah, and so on. In this book, because this is Kevin's story, this source is referred to as God. If you find the vocabulary off-putting, substitute a descriptor consistent with your own spiritual framework. Regardless of the name or framework, we probably all agree that to have an experience of ourselves as a soul or spirit, however this is described, is essential to living a full and rich life.

When people have a direct experience of the divine and/or a comatose or deceased loved one as described in this book, they are profoundly affected. They move beyond a head-based, intellectual, primarily mental receptivity to a heart-based, emotional resonance with the experience. Love, death, consciousness, and transcendent connections are centerpieces in this story. You may find yourself bumping up against your beliefs as you encounter possibilities that may have previously seemed too magical or too fantastic to be true.

Jocelyn will share her experiences, thoughts, and feelings. I will also contribute some of my perspectives on the story. More importantly, I will highlight and clarify some key elements of the experiences you'll be reading about. While these experiences may seem to be specific to Kevin and Jocelyn, they are really part of a larger story which we all share. Experiences like these allow us to feel more deeply, love and connect more fully, and embrace both ourselves and others more completely.

I hope that you will be moved, inspired, and expanded by what you will read. I invite you to open your mind and your heart to allow yourself to become part of this extraordinary experience.

CHAPTER 4

"What's Happening?"

Jocelyn

When you hear the words "cancer" and "brain tumor" your world stops. That's how it was for us when our dream-like Hawaiian vacation turned into a nightmare. While we frantically packed our stuff for the flight home from Hawaii, we left Kevin at the hospital. Within an hour, we returned for him and found that he had been loaded up with anti-seizure medication. This meant that although Kevin was conscious, he was groggy and confused. When we rolled his wheelchair up to the plane, the airline personnel almost didn't let us board. What if he were to experience another seizure mid-flight over the Pacific?

Only after the flight crew talked with Kevin's emergency room doctor were we allowed to make the journey. A very nice family gave up their first-class seats so that Kevin could lie down for the trip home. Everyone was truly kind to us throughout the flight. I knew they were thinking what I would have been thinking—that they felt sorry for us but were relieved it wasn't one of them. I've often had those same thoughts myself when I see something bad happen to someone else. It was sobering to be on the receiving end of them.

Kevin had eventually fallen asleep on the return plane ride. When he woke up, he asked me what had happened. I told him he had a brain tumor, that we were going home, and that he was going to be okay—although I didn't really believe it, since in a twist of fate, his brother had died from the same thing. To me, a brain tumor pretty much sounded like the worst thing that could happen to anyone. I kept thinking that if Kevin had suffered the seizure an hour later, we would have been snorkeling and he would have sunk like a rock and died right then. It's odd how, in moments like that, you are grateful that even in a horrible situation, it isn't the absolute worst-case scenario.

Arriving back in Santa Barbara, within a few days we were at UCLA consulting with the head of neurosurgery. From the MRI, the neurosurgeon thought it was a low-grade brain tumor, surmised that it could be removed, and was of the opinion that Kevin would be okay for at least another decade.

Within a few weeks the surgery to remove the tumor got underway. Everything went off without a hitch, relatively speaking, and we were back home in four days. Half of Kevin's hair had been shaved off, exposing a huge gash with staples holding his scalp together. He looked like Frankenstein.

The next few days were actually kind of funny. Kevin was on a high dose of steroids to stop his brain from swelling, and I finally understood the expression about someone going "roidle" on you. Every little thing pissed him off, from something being out of place on a shelf to a benign comment someone made. Nobody could do anything right. It was comical in a way because Kevin was usually such an easygoing, laid-back guy. Not much ruffled him, and to see him grinding his teeth over a misplaced pencil added some much-needed humor to the situation.

I later learned that people on such a high dose of steroids after surgery can be violent, which requires them to be hospitalized and sedated. Looking back on it, I think we got off easy with his pissy comments about pencil placement.

CHAPTER 5

THE NEWS WAS NOT GOOD

Jocelyn

It took over a week to get the results from the biopsy after Kevin's surgery, and the news was not good. It was a higher-grade tumor than the doctors originally thought. "Anaplastic astrocytoma" they dubbed it, which is a grade three out of four.

I started searching online, and what I read scared me even more. On average a patient with that condition dies within three and a half years of diagnosis. When I pressed the doctor for how long he thought my husband might expect to live, he said that Kevin had a 50-50 chance of making it to five years. It wasn't "if" the tumor was going to come back, but "when."

A recurrence of the tumor would most likely be in a worse form, the doctor explained, adding that dying from brain cancer was "not pretty." Kevin knew this firsthand because when he was 19, he had watched his 17-year-old brother die from the same cause.

Kevin didn't want to tell our children or anyone else about the type of tumor he had or his prognosis. He felt certain he was going to live longer than five years, and he didn't want people to worry or treat him like he was dying. Had it been me, I don't know what choice I would have made in that situation, but it wasn't my choice to make. I respected his decision, even if I didn't necessarily agree with it. We simply told our children that Kevin was fine now, and that the doctors would keep an eye on him. We decided were his condition to change, we would tell them then. Looking back on it, I'm glad we handled it like that. The end would come soon enough.

Kevin had already started chemotherapy and was slated to start radiation, but he had to wait two months following the surgery before he could begin the radiation. At the end of the first month, he was feeling a lot better. With his hair growing back, he looked like his old self. When he expressed a desire to return to work, I was opposed to this. Whatever the future held, it seemed to me that he should just retire early so we could enjoy our time together as a family for as long as possible. Since he loved what he did for a living, Kevin didn't want to do this. For him, going back to work represented life returning to normal.

About a month after the surgery, he went back to his mediation law practice, embarking on radiation a month later. Since his driver's license had been revoked and would not be reinstated until he had been seizure-free for at least three months, I had to chauffeur him everywhere. After six weeks of radiation, his hair started to fall out. Because it fell out in perfect circles, it looked like he had crop circles on his head. He was tired all the time now and just wanted to sleep. I knew he couldn't keep working, no matter how greatly he enjoyed it. When he finally agreed, we sent out a letter to all of his clients, informing them that he was taking a medical leave of absence.

Because Kevin made his living by being the sharpest guy in the room, I didn't want to tell everyone he had brain cancer. If people knew there was an egg-sized hole in his head, I thought they would think his abilities were diminished. In truth, at this point I honestly didn't think he would ever go back to work.

Kevin's surgery had changed him. Not in a negative way, but he was definitely different. He didn't see it, but the rest of us did. It was as if all his personality traits had been magnified. He was always a sentimental guy, but now he was more sentimental than ever. He always liked things to be orderly, and he was even more this way now. I later found out that this is a common side effect of brain surgery. Even though Kevin was somewhat different from the way he had always been, at his core he was still the man I had loved for over twenty years.

After the radiation treatment was over and his hair grew back, Kevin wanted to start back to work again. I was concerned people wouldn't want to hire him. Even though we had tried to keep his condition private, word had gotten out. Thankfully, my fears proved unfounded. Once he announced that he was going back to work, Kevin was busy again. Life was relatively normal, at least on the exterior.

CHAPTER 6

Every Minute Is Precious

Jocelyn

Living with and loving someone who is terminally ill is among life's most stressful situations. You are acutely aware that every minute that passes is one less you have to share. Every moment becomes precious.

While it's true that we all know we are going to die, when you know that the day is coming within a certain timeframe, it changes your perception of death. No longer way off in the future, it becomes more like an appointment on your calendar the following month.

Brain cancer is unlike other forms of cancer. With most cancers, the longer you are in remission, the better your chances are for avoiding a recurrence. The opposite is true of brain cancer. The longer you go cancer-free, the less time you have until it strikes again. Picture your life as a ruler. Every fraction of an inch you move from left to right, the closer you come to the end of the ruler. Knowing this, I was determined to make whatever time my husband had left the best it could be.

I couldn't escape the sense that Kevin's death was hanging over us, which meant I was just waiting for the other shoe to drop. Kevin didn't feel this way. He loved his life so much that he even felt grateful, almost blessed, that this had happened to him, since it enabled him to appreciate everything so much more. Determined to make every day worthwhile, he loved everyone more deeply.

Every two months after the first surgery, we returned to UCLA for an MRI and to meet with the neuro-oncologist. I was always a stressed-out nervous wreck, whereas Kevin wasn't concerned at all. We used to make a date night out of our visits, going down the night before his appointment, staying in a nice hotel, having a peaceful and kid-free dinner together for a change, and simply enjoying the time alone with one another.

I always sat right next to Kevin with my head resting on his legs while the MRI machine scanned his head. A mirror above his head enabled him to see me. Though I was always a teary mess, he would squeeze my hand, his eyes smiling as he did so. Afterwards, as we sat in the waiting room awaiting our consultation with the neuro-oncologist, I observed those around us in their various stages of the disease. This was always scary to me since I knew that one day Kevin and I would walk out of the hospital and things would no longer be okay.

Kevin's MRIs were fine until June 2013, almost three and a half years to the day after he was first diagnosed. When the oncologist walked into the examination room, I could tell from the look on his face that he was upset. We felt that Dr. Albert Lai had become a friend. In the two months since his previous MRI, Kevin had developed a rather large tumor in the same location as the original tumor.

When Dr. Lai informed us of what had transpired, Kevin looked at me and said simply, "I'm sorry, Joc" (pronounced "Joss"). It was so typical of him to be more worried about me than himself.

We looked over the MRI together as Dr. Lai explained that because of the location of the tumor, surgery might not be an option. He planned to consult with the neurosurgeon, and we would then decide what to do. He thought Kevin had a year left at best.

Telling our children that Kevin's cancer had returned was almost worse than informing them of the original tumor, since this time we knew their father wasn't going to be around much longer. He wouldn't live to see his youngest son finish junior high. He wouldn't see our kids get married or know what it was like to have grandchildren. He was only 59.

After consulting with the neurosurgeon, Kevin decided to have as much of the tumor removed as possible, along with restarting chemotherapy. The doctors speculated that taking these steps might gain him more time. With the tumor excised, his remaining time might also be of a higher quality. Although the original surgery had gone well, the second surgery wasn't without risk. A small percentage of the time, people didn't wake up. But this was usually if they had additional health issues such as hypertension, diabetes, or heart disease. Kevin was a tall and skinny vegetarian in great health other than having a brain tumor.

Surgery was scheduled for July 10, 2013. Since half of his head was going to be shaved, we decided to shave his whole head beforehand. I actually thought he looked cool with a shaved head. Because his hands were expected to swell up during the surgery, he asked me to take his wedding ring. I wear it to this day. He removed the cross he always wore from his neck and asked me to give it to one of our children to wear until he could wear it again himself. Because we didn't want to put them through the trauma of waiting anxiously throughout the somewhat lengthy procedure, the children were scheduled to arrive just before he was out of surgery.

Kevin was smiling at me when he went into surgery. "Everything will be fine," he reassured me. "But just in case it isn't, tell the kids I love them and am proud to be their father." He particularly wanted me to tell Chris, our oldest, who was struggling with drug addiction, that he knew he would grow up to be a fine man.

The surgery lasted several hours, following which the surgeon informed us that it had gone according to plan. But when we entered the recovery room, several nurses were gathered around Kevin's bed, gently shaking his shoulder and urging, "Wake up, Kevin." They told me he had been waking up, but each time seemed to lose consciousness.

Initially this didn't seem unusual. "You talk to him, and see if you can wake him up," one of the nurses suggested to me. But I couldn't wake him either. When they called for a doctor, I experienced my first inkling that something was wrong. Observing that one of Kevin's pupils was dilated, the doctor confirmed that something was seriously wrong—most likely bleeding in his brain.

By this time our children were in the hallway. "You should bring them in," the hospital staff urged. "There's a possibility your husband could die within the next several minutes." Shortly after the children entered the room, Kevin was wheeled away for a brain scan. The scan revealed that an artery had ruptured. "Massive hemorrhagic stroke" were the words used. They took him back into surgery to stop the bleeding.

I didn't realize it at the time, but this was the beginning of the end.

CHAPTER 7

AN EXCEPTIONAL HUMAN BEING

Jocelyn

When Kevin was diagnosed with brain cancer at 56, I was scared. Scared for him, scared for me, and scared for our children. But more than that, I was mad. Mad at the universe for inflicting such a horrible disease on such a wonderful person, furious at a God I didn't really even believe in.

I couldn't help asking myself, why do the worst things seem to happen to the best people? Why do the wife-beating, dog-kicking assholes of the world seem to go through life unscathed, other than the occasional consequence of their own bad choices? Yet people who live their lives enriching those around them often have the worst things happen to them.

With the odd exception, everyone says nice things about someone after they die—even when there are other things that might be said about them. But no one needed to cross their fingers behind their back when they said nice things about Kevin.

In reality he was truly an exceptional human being. Everyone loved him—and that's no exaggeration.

I can honestly say that I never knew anyone who had anything other than the most wonderful things to say about Kevin. He was smart, funny, successful, generous, handsome, and loyal to a fault. But more than that, he was kind—kinder than I often thought he should be. Way kinder than I ever was; he was kinder than any person I knew.

Because it was an integral part of his nature to "do unto others as you would have them do unto you," Kevin's kindness and empathy permeated everything he did. When homeless people asked him for money, not only did he generally give it to them, he looked them in the eyes and shook their hands—just like he would a business professional in a suit. I always kept hand sanitizer at the ready, because the hand that Kevin shook was usually filthy, given that the individual clearly hadn't bathed in weeks. "Is it really necessary to shake their hands?" I asked on more than one occasion. His answer was always the same. They were human beings just like himself, which meant they deserved to be treated with dignity no matter their circumstances.

On Wednesday evenings, Kevin volunteered at the Rescue Mission, serving food to the homeless, then staying for the worship service. Were it me, I would have just given an annual contribution. To Kevin's way of thinking, just giving money might be helpful, but he saw it as a hollow contribution. To him, that wasn't what service was about. On Saturday mornings he rose early, driving our old minivan to local stores that donated food for families and delivering it to the homeless shelter. His circuit included several stores. Only when the van was packed to the roof did he drop the goods at the shelter. Home before I'd finished my coffee, week after week I saw how he really was happiest when he was helping others.

Kevin's father lived in Santa Barbara during the last few years of his life. A resident of an assisted care facility, he suffered from dementia. Before we located the appropriate facility, he stayed with us for a few months. His dementia was so severe that he didn't recognize our children, or often me, and sometimes even his own son. Once he was in the care facility, Kevin visited every single day even if it was only for 15 minutes, stopping either on his way to work or on his journey home. Sometimes his dad didn't even know it was Kevin who was visiting until he reminded him, "I'm your son."

Since I felt certain my father-in-law forgot about the visit the instant Kevin walked out the door, I thought it was unnecessary for him to visit every single day—especially as, increasingly, his father failed to recognize him. But Kevin said that even if his dad didn't know it was him, he was sure he enjoyed the visit. Often his dad would be in the lobby, staring into space, waiting for his daily visitor. Kevin felt that if he were in that situation, he would want his son to visit as often as he could. So he did, every day. After Kevin died and I went to see his dad, he didn't recognize me and didn't even remember he had a son named Kevin.

Kevin was such a nice guy, it seemed an odd choice of profession for him to be a lawyer. I'm a lawyer too, and were you to meet me, you would probably think I fit the stereotype perfectly. In his early forties Kevin decided to shift his practice from litigation to mediation, and the change suited him perfectly. He spent his days helping people resolve their cases instead of going to trial, and he was a natural at it. While he was successful professionally, what mattered to him above all else was helping people resolve conflicts. I believe the reason he was so successful was that people felt he really heard them, understood their struggles, and truly wanted to help them get past what they were going through.

While things were always great between the two of us, our lives weren't perfect by any means. We had the usual ups and downs with the kids when they were younger. When our oldest son Chris became addicted to drugs, our lives were turned upside down. It was the first thing Kevin talked about when he woke up and the last thing on his mind as he fell asleep. If someone you love is struggling with addiction, you know what I'm talking about. For one of your children to be an addict is one of the worst things for any parent to endure. Not only was Chris homeless, skinny, smelly, and sick, there was nothing we could do to help him. We tried everything that most people in our situation try, but nothing worked. Twice we had to rush Chris to the emergency room when an overdose left him barely breathing. It was a living nightmare. While I know it was our son that was sick, we suffered right along with him. For Kevin not only to have brain cancer, but to have a child with a disease that could easily kill him, and almost did, only further supported my conviction that there couldn't be a God or higher power. Kevin deserved neither to be sick nor to have his son be sick.

The surgery that was intended to make the last year of Kevin's life better had gone horribly wrong. As he hung between life and death, his situation seemed like the worst possible cosmic joke being played on the last person on earth to deserve it. I felt that Kevin and I were being punished in some way. How could there possibly be a loving God, as Kevin believed, when someone like him was suffering in the way he was?

CHAPTER 8

THE LONGEST 26 DAYS OF MY LIFE

Jocelyn

By August 5, 2013, about three weeks after surgery, Kevin was a train wreck and I had lived through the longest and most grueling 26 days of my life. Everything that could possibly go wrong did, with each day bringing worse news.

Kevin never really woke up from surgery, only mumbling a word here and there. At best, he'd give me a hand squeeze or a pat on the back when I put his arm around me. He was there somewhere, trying to communicate. Several surgeries and more procedures later, there was no progress. The doctors had no idea why he wasn't waking up. They had done CT scans and MRIs, all of which appeared fine—and yet Kevin was still comatose.

The situation was beyond bleak. I felt not just overwhelmed but panicked and stressed-out beyond comprehension. I slept in Kevin's hospital bed with him every night, even when he was in the ICU, carefully positioning myself under and over all the wires, cords, and tubes that were keeping him alive. Because he was running a fever, he slept on a cooling mattress, which is basically like sleeping on a bed of ice. The nurses came in and out throughout the night, which meant I slept in 15- or 20-minute increments. After 26 days like this, my own body was killing me. Still hoping Kevin might wake up, I had no desire to leave him lest I miss it.

The neurosurgical team came in every morning around 6:00 a.m. to evaluate Kevin for any sign that he was awakening, but he wasn't. Once they left, I walked to the hotel where our children had essentially been living since everything went south. After taking a shower and downing a cup of coffee in the cafeteria, I returned to the hospital room. Once a day, when someone else could sit with Kevin, I left briefly to cram as much food in my mouth as I could.

One day while I was gone briefly, the nurse left Kevin's room in the ICU to care for someone else. During that time, his blood pressure and temperature spiked. Because of all the surgeries on his brain, it was essential that his blood pressure remain low in case another artery should burst. While the nursing staff were great, they couldn't be with him 24/7, so I invested a small fortune to provide Kevin with his own private ICU nurse. I wanted to do everything I could, in any way I could, to give him the best possible chance of recovering.

I wouldn't say I'm a control freak, but I definitely control what I can. The times in my life when things were out of my control and couldn't be fixed by using my intelligence or sheer willpower frustrated the hell out of me. The situation with Kevin was so completely out of my control. Despite doing everything I could, I felt I was failing miserably. Still, I wasn't about to give up. If I could have kept Kevin alive by sheer force of will, he would be here today.

I felt like a warrior in a life-or-death struggle to save someone more important to me than myself. And I was losing, losing badly.

CHAPTER 9

ALL OUT OF HOPE

Jocelyn

Following the initial surgery, my sister Vicky had mentioned several times that I should ask Catherine to do a writing for me. She had been the recipient of many writings over the years, drawing comfort and insight from them.

"I don't want to do that," I answered each time.

"At least let her pray with you," Vicky insisted, adding that Catherine was a prayer chaplain at her church.

If there was a God, this God was pretty low on my list of favorite people at the time. In truth, I didn't want to have anything to do with him.

By August 5, 2013, I was both all out of hope and all out of ideas on what to do next. Ever since I turned 25, every significant decision I made came as a result of careful consideration and discussion with Kevin. Now I found myself having to make life-and-death decisions on my own on a daily basis—decisions affecting the man who was the love of my life.

Since I was at the end of my rope, I figured there was no harm in giving the writing a go. Catherine and I agreed to a call later that evening. Vicky planned to stay with Kevin in his hospital room while I went to the hotel so I could talk on a landline. On the rare occasions I had interacted with Catherine over the years, she had struck me as an intelligent, witty, and pretty normal person. Still, I had no idea what to expect from one of her writings.

As I walked to the hotel, it occurred to me that desperate times call for desperate measures. I was way beyond desperate.

CHAPTER 10

Maybe God Can Help

Catherine

"Jocelyn isn't into any of this stuff," Vicky warned me, "so I don't know what you can do. But maybe God can somehow help her."

I thought perhaps I would just pray with her. But when I mentioned praying, Vicky cautioned, "Oh, she isn't religious at all. I don't think she'd want to do that."

I sat down at a large, carved antique desk at 9:30 p.m., fairly late for a writing session, but that hour worked for Jocelyn. I awaited her call. I never know what to expect when I do a writing, but even though I was on vacation in Washington State with my family, I had agreed to do what I could to help.

When the phone rang, Jocelyn sounded exhausted and apprehensive. I figured she had to be at her wits' end under the circumstances. We made small talk and I expressed sympathy for her and her family. When I offered to pray with her, she snapped, "No. I don't need the prayer thing. I just want you to do whatever that thing is you do that Vicky told me about."

I gave my usual disclaimer: "I don't know what's going to happen, but I'll get a pen and paper and we can try. Okay?"

It's my belief that if someone can find me so off the grid, God has arranged it. When I do writings, I step out of the way and let whatever God has intended just happen. I usually don't know details or the life history of most of the people for whom I write, only their names. Over the years, I have established friendships with a few people for whom I have written regularly, but that isn't typical. Most people who ask for my help are referred to me and are complete strangers.

When I write, I'm fully present. I write at a rapid-fire pace. People often ask me how I receive this information. After almost 30 years, I'm still not quite sure myself how it works and therefore I can't explain it. I experience it as my own thought process, but with a distinct energy that I sense. I've relinquished the need for an explanation.

I've witnessed many miracles through the writings and have learned that all I need to do is show up and offer to be of service. The connection comes from the God who lives in and through all of us, whether we are in this human realm or another. So when Jocelyn asked me to "do my thing," I wasn't sure what that was going to look like. I got out my paper and a pen, readying myself for God to give Jocelyn whatever message she was supposed to receive.

First Writing

August 5, 2013

CHAPTER 11

THE SOUL KNOWS

Kevin, Jocelyn, and Catherine

Note: We have included our reactions and comments to the writing. Catherine's are in *sans serif* and Jocelyn's in *italics*.

I could hear Catherine writing over the phone. She stopped after a few minutes and read me what she had written:

GOD: The windows are all foggy and the sunlight seems distant in the mist. From a corner, there is an opening in the distance and a radiant blue light emerges—turquoise and golden, a washing and fading. But the eye need not be open to see what the soul intuits innately. There are the shafts aplenty, indiscernible but not unpleasant or unsettling. For the soul has its own comforting agents that tell you that your illumination comes from within you. Trust the senses. Soul knows the way. The foggy mists surround the consciousness, but the soul knows it isn't the outer focus but the inner knowing that counts. The windows, though foggy, can't eclipse what the soul knows, speaks, and directs innately. The process of drawing inward does not connote vacancy, but a more soulful inhabitation.

The God introductions are always different, yet most revealing. They establish a theme unique to each writing. In this writing, God seemed to be saying that Kevin's level of consciousness was still illumined, though perhaps not in the mind. His inner reality and knowing were unaffected by what he was going through.

God has elaborated in so many writings about the ways our mind and thoughts actually hinder our awareness of soul. Although intuition has been discussed in other writings I've done, what's offered here is so much deeper—that "soul intuits innately."

This "soulful inhabitation" is neither perceived, achieved, nor preserved through the mind. In his so-called unconsciousness, Kevin was more soul-conscious than most of us.

Specifically, it is through our soul that intuition arises. Birthrights give us a body, whereas soul rights give us access to this place of inner contact with ourselves and the innate wisdom we all possess.

CHAPTER 12

I'M STILL HERE

MAN'S VOICE: I'm still here, I'm still here, I'm still here!

JOCELYN: Is it Kevin?

KEVIN: Of course it's me. But this is so unbelievable. I've been trying to let you know I'm okay.

> *All I could think was, "Oh my God!!" (No pun intended.) Could it really be Kevin? I wanted to believe it, but I didn't know if it was possible. I mean, Kevin was comatose. How could he communicate? I was so hoping it was him.*

JOCELYN: Where are you?

KEVIN: It's not a place. It's more these sensations of light and electricity. I don't recognize it. I've never been here before. I hear you, but I don't see you. I feel your breath. You smell like the wind, but I don't recognize this place. I'm trying to reach out and let you know I'm okay, and yet I can't seem to find a way out of here. It's not awful, just confusing that I can't find a way to articulate and connect with you. What is this? It's not only confusing but intriguing. Is this a long, long dream and I have been unable to wake myself out of it? Is this myself in my dream speaking for me? It's all so confusing, and I hear you clearly now. (*Catherine spoke to me here.*)

KEVIN: Who is this other voice? Is this part of my dream too?

JOCELYN: You had the brain surgery, and that went fine. In the recovery room an artery tore in your head and it's been all downhill from there. You are really sick, and I am so scared! I miss you so much, and you aren't waking up. I stay with you all the time. I sleep in the hospital bed with you at night. I only leave you in the morning to go take a shower and change, then once later in the day to get something to eat. I'm just so scared and I don't know what to do!

KEVIN: This is some post-surgical dream, right? But we were just together. I wouldn't ever leave you like this. Is this my dream?

JOCELYN: You'd never do it by choice. It's not a dream, honey.

KEVIN: So you are telling me I'm not in this confusing place? I'm lying somewhere and you're not eating but only once a day? Where are the kids? Who's with them? What's Will doing?

> Our youngest son, Will, had just turned thirteen a few weeks before Kevin's surgery.

JOCELYN: The kids come back and forth to Los Angeles and stay at the hotel. Vicki and Sue (*close friends*) take care of Will when he's in Santa Barbara. They've been great.

KEVIN: No way! Are you joking? I'm dreaming. This is not possible, Joc. What are you saying? I know what you're describing, but what's wrong with me?

> Up to this point, Kevin hadn't said anything that was really personal to us. I didn't really know Catherine, although my sister Vicky did. Vicky could have told Catherine the names of our kids, but when he called me "Joc," which is what Kevin

always called me, I started to believe it was really him. There was only one way to find out whether I was really talking to Kevin.

JOCELYN: What's the last thing you remember, sweetie?

KEVIN: I remember before going into surgery, reaching up and taking Linda's hand and saying, "Thank you for doing this, Linda."

At this point, I nearly fell off my chair. That was almost verbatim what the surgeon told me Kevin said to her before he went into surgery. I knew beyond a shadow of doubt that I was talking to Kevin. There was no way Catherine could have known what Kevin said to the surgeon.

CHAPTER 13

THIS HAS TO BE A DREAM

KEVIN: But then I thought I was just in this anesthesia place. So if I'm hearing this correctly, you're saying I'm still in the hospital, you and the kids are shuttling back and forth, and you're on Kevin watch and a new form of starvation diet.

> *This was actually a pretty funny comment from him. I have been on one diet or another since I had children. Whenever I started a new one, Kevin would always say that I was on some new form of starvation diet. I laughed at that. I felt like we were talking in a way we hadn't since the shit hit the fan following the surgery.*

JOCELYN: After the surgery, an artery tore in your head. It's called a hemorrhagic stroke. You immediately went back into surgery so they could fix the artery. Then they had to insert a drain in your brain to remove the blood caused by the stroke. They intubated you three times in one day, which meant you had to be put on a ventilator. They said that because your throat was so swollen, you needed a breathing tube. Otherwise your throat would swell shut and you would suffocate.

After a few weeks, because you weren't waking up, they thought that putting a shunt in to drain the fluid from your ventricles into your body might fix it. They thought that the fluid in your ventricles was putting pressure on your brain, which would explain why you were still comatose. Even after they inserted the shunt, you still weren't waking up. The shunt just went into one ventricle, which meant the ventricles were draining unevenly. So they did a fifth surgery, this time to run a tube in between the ventricles so they would drain evenly.

That all took place during the last month. You were supposed to be home in four days, and it's been almost a month. Despite all the tubes and drains, you still aren't waking up. Plus, you keep getting pneumonia. To prevent this you have to undergo breathing treatments, which help expand your lungs. You're so sick, and I'm so scared.

I hated telling him everything that had happened. I didn't realize he had no idea what he had been through. While I was telling him all the things that had gone wrong, I was thinking to myself how bad it sounded. Reciting everything all at once made it seem even worse than it had at the time.

KEVIN: A month? It's been a month? That's not possible. Can I talk now?

JOCELYN: No. Well, sort of. You mumble.

KEVIN: Am I awake?

JOCELYN: Not really. Sort of, at times. And you drool.

KEVIN: Oh crap!

I was going for a lighthearted moment here. Before Kevin underwent this surgery, he told me he didn't want to end up like one of those old men, slumped over and drooling in his chair.

KEVIN: Did you say "tube"?

JOCELYN: They had to put in a trach tube and also a feeding tube.

KEVIN: What?!

JOCELYN: You needed a breathing tube, and after a few weeks they said they had to take it out because it was contributing to your pneumonia. They had to cut a hole in your throat and put in a trach tube. Another tube in your nose led to your stomach to feed you. They took that out because they said it was uncomfortable to have it in long-term, so they put a feeding tube directly into your stomach. I'm so sorry …

> *The doctors had wanted to put in both a trach tube and a feeding tube about a week after the first surgery, but I didn't want them to do that. I kept hoping Kevin would wake up and it would prove unnecessary. I didn't want them cutting any more holes in him and performing additional procedures that would make his condition seem more permanent than I was willing to admit.*

KEVIN: Mr. Potato Head.

> *Kevin always had a great sense of humor. I knew he was trying to be lighthearted over his condition, but I hated that he was comparing himself to a toy with missing parts of his head.*

> Though I facilitate many connections for people, most of the time the person on the other side is dead and has some awareness of what happened to them. Kevin was alive, yet he had no idea about all the procedures done to help him. He said he thought he was dreaming. I winced when I heard the litany of all this man had gone through. It was horrible. Then, in all of this darkness, he

came up with a way to lighten it. Sensing Jocelyn's overwhelmed state in view of his growing problems, instead of being angry or scared, he made her laugh. Although his body was suffering, it appeared he wasn't feeling any pain.

JOCELYN: It's so good to talk to you! You do say little things. You say, "Love you" or "Love you, son."

Even in his comatose state, when I would say, "Love you, Kevie" (a nickname I often used for him), he replied, "Love you," or "Love you, son" to Will or Chris. He often called Will or Chris "son." He was from the 50s and was formal in that 1950's "Leave it to Beaver" way.

KEVIN: This just seems too fantastic a story. So how am I able to talk to you and hear you so clearly now?

Like other coma patients in writings, Kevin indicated that he could hear better. Although I had never thought about it before, apparently my gift allows not only for me to connect with other people's energy, but somehow amplifies their ability to receive messages.

JOCELYN: Do you remember Vicky's friend, Catherine?

KEVIN: Oh yeah, a little. I remember she was involved in her church and told me about a book. What's she got to do with this?

One day, Kevin told me that he had run into Vicky and Catherine having lunch. They talked about a spiritual book that Catherine was reading. Kevin was always reading a spiritual book.

JOCELYN: Vicky and I told you she had a gift.

KEVIN: Boy, I guess she does. I didn't think that was funny. Oh my gosh! This is something I'd hear about at my seminars.

Kevin went to religious seminars more frequently after he was sick. He belonged to prayer groups and met weekly with friends to pray and to study various religious texts.

JOCELYN: I have a bunch of questions. I want to know what you want me to do. I don't really know what you want. Do you know whether you're going to recover from this?

KEVIN: I didn't know I hadn't. What you are telling me isn't what I want for my family. If this isn't a dream and it's all real, you know what I want.

JOCELYN: I actually don't. Albert said you had about a year …

We had talked before about how Kevin wanted me to handle the end stage of his life, but in my mind this wasn't the end.

KEVIN: I didn't want all of you to have to witness in graphic detail my deterioration.

JOCELYN: You told me that.

KEVIN: But you are saying a month has gone by and I'm full of tubes, and you are keeping a bedside vigil and the kids are going back and forth. No, this falls in the realm of our discussion. Dream or no—that's clear. Now, I know we were expecting complications, but this is more than complications. Come on, Joc! Listen to yourself—brain bleed? Respirator? Those are words that should never pass anybody's lips. Shunts that drain where? This has to be a dream.

CHAPTER 14

A BEYOND-SALVAGEABLE SITUATION

JOCELYN: I'm so sorry I let them do so many things to you, but I think you are slowly getting better. We've had some good news in the last week. The MRI from a few days ago looks fine. You had a spinal tap because the right side of your face was drooping and your right eye wouldn't close. They thought that maybe the cancer had spread to your spinal canal, but it hasn't. Each time a decision had to be made, I made the best decision under the circumstances. I'm so sorry, Kevie. I had no idea it was going to turn out like this.

> *I was feeling bad at this point for agreeing to so many invasive procedures. It all just snowballed, with one thing after another going wrong, and the only way to fix whatever it was just became more and more invasive. I had no idea that it would end up as such a cumulative mess.*

> Jocelyn had only done all she could for Kevin out of love. She sounded contrite and defeated. Clearly she hated delivering all of this bad news to him. It hadn't dawned on her yet that Kevin hadn't said he was in any pain.

KEVIN: No apologies, please. And you say there are other problems? Isn't the list long enough? Other problems? Incredible. Are we really having this discussion? Spinal tap? And you say there's some good news in all of this? Do you hear what you are saying? How is that good? I'm not being confrontational.

JOCELYN: You are never confrontational.

KEVIN: No, I mean you are outlining a beyond-salvageable situation.

JOCELYN: That's not true. You are actually improving. Every day you are starting to wake up a little. When I reach down, you pat and scratch my back.

KEVIN: It's an automatic response. Years of training. We need clarity in this conversation.

JOCELYN: I have some choices to make. You are going to be released to acute rehab if you are more awake. If not, they want you to go to skilled nursing, which I won't agree to. I'd rather bring you home.

> *Looking back at this time, I realize how in denial I was. I simply couldn't face up to the fact Kevin was dying. There was nothing I could do to prevent it. It was like the frog you put in cold water then heat the water slowly to a boil. The frog doesn't jump out. But if you throw the frog into boiling water, it jumps out instantly. I was the frog in the cold water heating up, and Kevin was the frog thrown into the boiling water. He could see the situation more clearly than I could.*

KEVIN: I want it to be easiest on you. I want it to be as normal as possible for my family. That's what I want, and you're saying normal is probably the most improbable end state. I'm not scared. I'm not in pain, but I am clear that this is not what I want all of you to have to go through. I'm not equivocating even the slightest.

JOCELYN: I don't know what "equivocating" means.

I actually didn't know what he meant by that. My brain was on overload at this point.

KEVIN: You always out-gunned me intellectually and now you're playing stupid? Come on. I must be dreaming. "Equivocating" is what I made a living at for years. I'm sure and steady and unwavering that this isn't how I want to be kept. I'm so sorry. It seems it's left up to you. And in your so-loving but so-dictatorial way, you've taken on so much more than either of us could have anticipated. Where am I—am I still in L.A.?

JOCELYN: You are at UCLA in the hospital. There's an acute rehab here and that's where I was planning on taking you after your release from the hospital. The other option is a rehab facility in Santa Barbara.

KEVIN: It's not okay. Why can't you transport me home?

JOCELYN: I can. I can totally do that. Is that your first choice?

KEVIN: How am I physically? What you describe is a train wreck.

In the legal field, when someone has multiple physical problems, they are called a train wreck. I knew what he was talking about.

JOCELYN: I knew you'd say that. You're pretty thin, kind of skinny.

Because Kevin hadn't been able to swallow, they had been feeding him solely through a feeding tube. He was 6' 2", and about 190 pounds when he went into the hospital for surgery. He was down to about 160 pounds at this point and looked really skinny.

KEVIN: What? Maybe in the ninth grade. I don't need the descriptions. And start eating—you can't evaporate.

JOCELYN: I'm eating pickles and drinking beer whenever I can.

> *My favorite food is pickles and my favorite drink is beer.*
> *It was a joke between us about my love of pickles and beer.*

KEVIN: I'd love to be there drinking with you. Maybe you could just put it in one of my tubes.

JOCELYN: I'll ask them if I can put it down your feeding tube.

KEVIN: Ah, the girl loves me! I know you do. But you have to also face facts, even if it's hard. So start with Santa Barbara rehab. Then if I don't progress, and I mean really, as in not this kind of intermediary state, I am really clear. You know I'm fully 100% ready and not afraid. So I say go for Santa Barbara rehab, but if rehab isn't possible, you have to accept it. It's not a failure. I've been ready and I'm accepting. You know I'm accepting. I've done my research—and I have no doubt, no hesitation, none whatsoever. I believe. I believe so strongly that this is a blip on the screen in some eternal channel, and you and I are going to be together regardless. Regardless! So stop being so darn positive and sugarcoating this. I say Santa Barbara rehab, but you have to set an exit date. You have to!

> *I didn't know Kevin, having only seen him once when I was with Vicky. I would later learn that he was a deeply spiritual man. The time to develop faith isn't at the eleventh hour, when we need it the most. He was "100% ready," "not afraid," and "ready and accepting." Even more, he was certain they'd be together again. This too has been echoed in countless writings I've done with deceased people—that loved ones are often reunited in the hereafter.*

JOCELYN: If you're not well enough to go to rehab, I'd much rather bring you home.

> *The way it works is that when you are in the hospital and comatose, you have two choices. If they think that rehab might help you regain more function, then you can go there. If they don't think you are a candidate for rehab, then you go to a skilled nursing facility—a nice name for a nursing home— where you essentially rot until you die. There was no way I was going to send Kevin to a skilled nursing facility. If I couldn't get him into rehab, I was going to bring him back home, hire nurses, and take care of him myself.*

CHAPTER 15

I'M BOUND FOR A DIFFERENT HOME

KEVIN: Location is immaterial to me. What matters is what's best for everyone—and if home is easier, then home it is. But this isn't to sidestep the central point, which is that I'm bound for a different home and it sounds like this is really the blue elephant in the room. Call it pink, I know you. But it's what we have, so I'd ask that you just set an exit date. If I'm not able to talk to you and engage as myself, then you need to move from rehab mode to release. I'm so sorry to have to be blunt, but if you are really telling me this horrific narrative—that I'm thin, can't move my face, have a tube to breathe and feed, it sounds pretty serious. And you have been with me all this time. Gee, I knew you were stubborn. But my God, you'd fistfight St. Peter if you thought you could win.

JOCELYN: I'm fighting for you, and I'm not about to give up. That's not an option for me.

KEVIN: But it is for me because it's not giving up. It's inevitable. But I know you don't want to hear it. It's like a negotiation settlement—I just want a drop date.

A mediator by profession, Kevin helped people negotiate settlements on their legal cases instead of going to trial. He was great at it.

JOCELYN: That's actually not my choice. You are not dying right now. You are comatose.

KEVIN: Are you kidding me? I'm only trying to outline some parameters for a date whereby if I'm not progressing, you let it be easy. Do I seem in pain?

JOCELYN: Sometimes. Your head hurts. They give you morphine or Vicodin for it.

KEVIN: It sounds like a college boy's weekend fantasy—our son's exactly. Sorry, I'm trying to make light because this is so overwhelming.

Kevin always kept his sense of humor. Our eldest son's addiction was our biggest worry in life.

JOCELYN: How are you? I don't care about myself, I only care about you.

KEVIN: So where does that leave my opinion about how I care about you? She Who Must Be Obeyed …

This was a joke between us. "She Who Must Be Obeyed" was from a movie and was slang for "My Wife Who Must Be In Charge." Kevin thought it was really funny and would sometimes call me "She Who Must Be Obeyed," then laugh at his own joke. He really was a goofball in a lot of ways.

KEVIN: It wasn't just funny, it was true.

JOCELYN: I know you say that with love in your heart.

KEVIN: Most definitely. I'm so full of love. I'm grateful for every second you have been in my life. Every second—up, down, upside down, it has all been you. If there was ever the slightest question about divine intervention, forget about it. We are so blessed to have had all this time—all this magic really. I'm pained that you are having to deal with this, and it sounds like without any thought of yourself. And okay, I give that right to you, but not our kids. Because like it or not, you're it—and if you go down, well, I'm not even entertaining it. You have to put yourself into a long-term care strategy. It's stupid not to.

JOCELYN: For you?

KEVIN: For you as well as me. Seems you qualify for a little rehab yourself about now.

> *At this point I was laughing. I used to tell him that going to rehab like the celebrities do in Malibu sounded like a great gig. They have private chefs and masseuses. They divide their day between yoga and lying on the beach. No commuting to work, doing laundry, cooking, cleaning, or shuttling kids around.*

KEVIN: It's good to hear you laugh.

JOCELYN: Well sweets, I have to decide whether to give you chemotherapy again pretty soon.

KEVIN: If I'm a vegetable, I don't want chemo.

JOCELYN: I don't want to not give you chemo if you have a chance of recovering from this. I would feel guilty.

> *The plan had always been for Kevin to start chemotherapy again after the surgery. The doctors had held off, waiting for him to improve. But if it was going to happen at all, it had to be started soon.*

KEVIN: It would probably kill me and that could be a win at this point. I'm not trying to be glib. I think you should do what you need for you. I don't want loose strings in your psyche. So sure, start chemo. Sounds like I wouldn't know the difference anyway. But it really seems like this is a losing hand, and no bluffing is getting us out of here. So if you need to decide, and if your conscience feels like it would leave you tormented if you don't, then do what you have to.

But this is derailing us from the central point, and I can't fathom it hasn't been arrived at yet. I'm either not getting better or just lingering. So I choose not to linger once it's clear. I don't mean at an emotional level for you, but at a factual level—the level of a truth too difficult to absorb. The most horrible truth, but the truth nonetheless. Then I want to go as easily as possible. Okay? That's our agreement.

No way was I going to make that agreement.

JOCELYN: You're getting a little better every day.

KEVIN: I just get flashes of sensations and electricity like shockwaves. I was thinking I was dreaming, so I sort of wasn't paying close attention. This sounds much more elaborate than post-anesthesia psychosis. I guess that would be preferable. I love you! You know that's the gift. That's the gravy. That's the blessing. Would that I were bionic, but I'm mortal—and even you, with all your tenacity and bulldoggedness, can't change mortality's way. So love me. And when the time comes, love me the hardest way. Because you know it's only a blink of an eye. Do those still work?

JOCELYN: Just your left eye. Both your eyes work, but you can't blink with your right eye.

We never knew why Kevin couldn't blink his right eye or
why the right side of his face drooped. It wasn't from the stroke,

because that affected only the left side of his body. Eventually the doctor had to sew Kevin's right eye shut to protect the cornea from damage. I hated that, because Kevin had beautiful blue eyes.

KEVIN: Sounds like they are pretty incompetent if they haven't figured it out.

JOCELYN: You do look kind of surprised and confused.

KEVIN: This is so unbelievable.

I realized now that all along Kevin had been gently leading Jocelyn to the obvious. In all her love and tending, she just couldn't hear it: Kevin was dying. As difficult as it was, she probably could only hear it from him. He knew her weaknesses and resistance. Like many people facing the death of a loved one, for whom all medical procedures have already failed, Jocelyn desperately clung to an empty whisper and echo of optimistic hope that Kevin would recover. Even as a shell of a man, Kevin was generous with his love, humor, wisdom, and honesty.

CHAPTER 16

DYING ISN'T A FAILURE

JOCELYN: Are you scared or anxious?

I was so worried Kevin would be scared or anxious, especially now he'd heard everything that was wrong with him. I knew I was.

KEVIN: No, I'm just perplexed. I'm not scared about dying. I'm complete with that. You aren't, but I am. Dying isn't a failure. It's a transition and it sounds like if things are as you say, it may be a godsend. I know that you see my dying as a failure, a loss, some big cheat. But I got the greatest payoff—I got you. We have our family. We did good, and you know I'm not about the kicking and screaming. I know I'm going somewhere, and I know that you'll come find me. Then it's just us, like always. Maybe you were my heaven prep school, with a mean nun occasionally.

I started laughing here at his "mean nun" comment. Even though the circumstances of our conversation were terrible, and even though I was hearing what he was saying through Catherine, it just felt like we were having a regular conversation.

JOCELYN: We laughed a lot.

KEVIN: Yes, we did. We amused ourselves. That's a gift.

There was an easy rhythm to their conversation. Jocelyn seemed more relaxed now, more accepting, less sullen.

JOCELYN: If I don't get to talk to you again, I'm sorry for any unkind thing you thought I ever did, even if I really didn't mean it.

KEVIN: If that's not a half-hearted apology, I don't know what is.

JOCELYN: I'm not as nice as you are.

KEVIN: Every good cop needs a bad one. No, you weren't unkind, but neither were you easy all the time. You stretched me in ways I couldn't imagine. You put fire in me, put passion in me. You inspired me and you still do. You make my heart race like it did in that parking lot. How's my heart, by the way?

The parking lot reference was just another example of something Catherine could know nothing about. Kevin was referring to our first date, which wasn't really a date. We were doing a work thing together, inspecting an oil platform where a worker was injured, followed by the individual's deposition. We spent the day together, and by the end neither of us wanted to go home. So we decided to watch the NBA finals (Lakers vs. Celtics of the Magic Johnson / Larry Bird era) and bet dinner on the outcome. Kevin lost the bet and we went to get Chinese food. After dinner he drove me back to the parking lot of our law firm, where we held hands and kissed in the car like teenagers. Every year that we were in town on that day, we went to the same Chinese restaurant, sat at the same table (where he always had flowers waiting), then went to that parking lot and kissed like teenagers all over again.

JOCELYN: Your heart is fine.

KEVIN: Thank God something works.

JOCELYN: You're not as bad as it sounds. You're in an in-between state.

KEVIN: Waking up shouldn't be the measure of the quality of life. So remember the negotiation of a drop date. It's what I need agreement on.

> *Kevin always liked agreements for everything—study hours for the kids, bedtimes, curfews, TV watching times. He brokered agreements for a profession, and he was always seeking them in our home. Because we often ended up breaking them, I hated making agreements about anything.*

JOCELYN: What do you have in mind?

KEVIN: You say we are thirty days out now.

JOCELYN: It will be four weeks this Thursday.

KEVIN: Okay, what do you think? Ninety days?

JOCELYN: No. It wouldn't change anything I do. When you're not ready to be here, then it's your time. I'm going to take care of you until then.

KEVIN: But it sounds like medical intervention limits my choice points too.

JOCELYN: That's true, it does.

KEVIN: So how is that fair?

JOCELYN: How we got to this point is that one thing happened after another. I made the best decision at the time as each thing occurred.

KEVIN: That's what I'm asking you—to realize that at some point I don't want to be kept alive if I'm not living.

JOCELYN: I understand that.

Nobody wants to be kept alive if they aren't living. The reason people make living wills is to prevent this from happening. The problem with those living wills is that, in a situation like Kevin's where you make small incremental decisions along the way, you find yourself a month down the road keeping someone alive who isn't really living, even when this isn't something they ever wanted.

KEVIN: I'm saying if I'm not better in sixty days. Is that comfortable?

JOCELYN: How about ninety?

KEVIN: We can revisit it. Ninety it is.

JOCELYN: I don't have direct access to you to revisit it.

KEVIN: That's why I'm trying to get some loose terms drafted.

At this, I found myself wondering what Catherine must have thought of us. Can you tell we're both lawyers?

JOCELYN: Ninety days from today, if you aren't better and medical things come up, I won't do it if that's your wish. Though it doesn't seem long enough.

KEVIN: Because you will never be ready.

JOCELYN: It's true.

KEVIN: But you're my partner, so I'm relying on you. You never back down, but something like this isn't a salvage operation. It's about living. So ninety days from Thursday. If I can get a signature. I'm not sure, I know you're already strategizing.

He was right. I was already thinking of ways to circumvent this agreement. No way was I going to let him go in ninety days.

They countered each other so quickly that it was hard for me to keep up with writing down all their terms. Even though I'm married to an attorney and I studied communication, these two were almost comical were it not for the topic of their negotiation.

CHAPTER 17

I AM A BLESSED MAN

JOCELYN: I'll do what you want. I really didn't know what you would want.

KEVIN: But you know, it's like my memory is hopeful. The night before surgery, holding you. The ride down to the hospital, listening to James Taylor. Your face. See, it's all so rich. I am a blessed man. I love you beyond words, which is a good thing since apparently I can't speak now. But I'm still trained, so that even though I'm unconscious, I respond to all cues Jocelyn. I love you, and you know that whether I'm semi-unconscious or unconscious, the love isn't even going to change. If I stop breathing, I'll still love you.

On the ride down to UCLA, we listened to James Taylor in the car the whole way. He was one of our favorite musicians. The night before the surgery, we lay in bed and I had my head on his shoulder with his arm around me. It's how we fell asleep every night for the last 26 years. The night before the surgery, we talked the whole night, reminiscing about the life we'd shared together and the things we were going to do when he recovered. I'd thought about that day and night together a lot over the last month because it was the last good time we'd had together.

People are often so intimate during writings. I don't feel embarrassed or judgmental. I'm always moved by the human capacity to love. Kevin reassured Jocelyn that he would never stop loving her. I prayed she could receive it. It was so important for him to tell her all she meant to him and to thank her. I also wondered whether he had held on in order to say these things and absolve her of the guilt she might feel. Perhaps now that he had reassured her that their love was eternal, he might pass more easily.

JOCELYN: All those things you said about loving me, I say about you.

KEVIN: Yes. I never ever doubted for a second that your love is unwavering, undying. I'm a blessed man.

JOCELYN: Is there anything you want me to tell the kids?

KEVIN: If your dad could choose, he'd have chosen never to burden you with this. But dad doesn't get to choose. So I promise I'm going to start taking better care of myself. I will be eating two times a day. [*He was referring to the one-meal-a-day diet I had been on for the last month.*] And you know I'm serious about this, particularly for Will. It's important he doesn't see you getting ill yourself. That's why being in Santa Barbara seems a better option for me.

JOCELYN: I can do that.

KEVIN: Okay, whenever they say I'm transportable.

JOCELYN: It will be the end of this week.

KEVIN: If I die en route, then no second-guesses. Okay?

JOCELYN: Okay, but you won't.

KEVIN: I know I'm glory bound.

Kevin never doubted where he would be going when he died, but I didn't like him talking as though it was going to happen soon.

JOCELYN: You're not dying yet.

KEVIN: Whenever it is, I'm ready. I know you aren't, and that's okay. I'm not being dramatic.

JOCELYN: I do feel kind of cheated, and so do the kids.

To say I felt cheated was an understatement. I felt robbed— robbed of whatever quality time we would have enjoyed together had the surgery not been a complete disaster.

KEVIN: Yes, I know, I know. But let's not re-rake the gravel of what's been. I'm proud of each one of our kids. I know they'll do amazing things.

CHAPTER 18

LET'S DO AN EXPERIMENT

KEVIN: So, I'm asking you to tap my fingers. Let's experiment and see if I can tap back.

This sudden change of topic caught me off guard. I wasn't sure where he was going with this.

JOCELYN: I'm not with you in the room, Vicky is.

KEVIN: Yes, I know. I can smell her perfume.

Until the conversation turned to this finger tapping experiment, I thought Jocelyn was in Kevin's hospital room. I was a thousand miles away in Washington State.

I called my sister on her cell phone from my hotel room. I had the landline cradled against one ear and my cell phone against the other ear. My sister began telling me everything that was transpiring in the hospital room, while I also listened to Catherine in the other ear.

JOCELYN: I'm going to have Vicky tap your fingers. Are you going to tap back?

KEVIN: I'm going to try. I'm doing it! Hey, so this really does work. It's just for me to see how I can reach out. I know I'm doing it. I'm doing it!

JOCELYN: That's so bizarre.

KEVIN: I know! I'm trying to see whether I can wake myself up.

JOCELYN: Can you say something? How about you say "Joc"?

KEVIN: Why is she talking to me? [*Catherine was talking at the same time.*]

JOCELYN: Do you want to try?

KEVIN: Sure. I'd rather just say it. Well, be quiet, this takes concentration. I'm tapping my fingers again.

JOCELYN: Vicky says you are clutching her hand and tapping her fingers.

KEVIN: I know. It's hard to form words. But it seems it was a successful experiment. I'd much prefer you, but I hope you are eating while we're talking.

> This was a miracle. Jocelyn was ecstatic—and I'm sure she was also in shock, like I was. This man, I was told, was unconscious. Only an hour earlier he thought he was dreaming, and now he was tapping his fingers. I was so grateful they could have this experience.

JOCELYN: Most of the time you have your hand on my boob.

KEVIN: A comfort item.

JOCELYN: You were even doing that in front of Will.

KEVIN: Embarrassing.

> *I was laughing now. The whole time Kevin was in the hospital, even when he was comatose, he would always reach*

up my shirt and have his hand on my chest. The nurses and doctors thought it was really funny. I would joke that he must be okay if he could do that. Kevin was always a boob man, which is why even in the worst of times in the hospital when he wasn't really moving otherwise, he would put his hand on my chest. Old habits die hard.

JOCELYN: Anything else you want to talk about?

I felt like, at this point, we had covered pretty much everything. I knew what he wanted me to do going forward. It was really late, almost midnight, and I felt guilty for taking up so much of Catherine's time. Plus I really wanted to get back to the hospital to Kevin, because now he knew that he wasn't dreaming. Since I was hoping this would be the start of him recovering from this nightmare, I couldn't wait to get back to him.

KEVIN: Just let me thank you! I'm not sure how this worked, but I think now that I'm clear it's not a dream, I can try harder to move past it. That's why I wanted to try the experiment, to see if I really am able to knowingly communicate. Seems hopeful to me.

JOCELYN: I really think you can do this. You should try harder now that you know you aren't dreaming. I miss you.

KEVIN: So to recap, two meals a day. Santa Barbara move whenever it's the best option. Sixty days, and no more intervention. This is not a dream, and I do have the ability to communicate. We got to banter again and that is so delightful.

JOCELYN: I miss that.

Kevin always liked to summarize a plan whenever it had been finalized. He did it all the time. I don't know why he said sixty days, because I thought we had agreed on ninety.

KEVIN: Okay, thanks. I love you! I love you! And you know, regardless, we will always be together. I love you!

GOD: Go with God.

When the writing was over and I hung up the phone with Catherine, I just sat in the hotel chair stunned. I was actually able to connect with Kevin, which I wasn't expecting. I don't know what I was expecting from the writing, but it wasn't that. My sister had told me that Catherine could communicate with dead people, but Kevin wasn't dead, and I hadn't really believed Catherine could do this anyway. I mean, come on, someone who can actually talk to dead people? Not only was it amazing that I was able to talk to Kevin, but what was really weird is that when I was in the middle of the writing, I felt like he and I were having a regular back-and-forth conversation. I know it sounds strange, and it is. But when you are having the experience, it doesn't seem strange or unusual at all.

Jocelyn was animated and hopeful. God knows the precise words to comfort people in these writings, and the way to ease their burdens, transform, and liberate them. God usually has a longer conclusion other than "Go with God" at the end of the writings. I found it odd that this one didn't. But Jocelyn was so eager to get off the phone and race to Kevin's bedside now that he was waking up. I didn't know then, nor could I have imagined, that this would be the first of many conversations.

Though I had been clear with Jocelyn upfront that I didn't know whether Kevin would talk during the writing, I didn't feel God would put us together if it wasn't in the realm of possibility. I had done other writings connecting a recipient with their loved one in a coma, so I knew it was possible.

The deceased and people in comas usually share a detail so specific that only the recipient knows about it. When this happens, the recipient no longer engages in wishfully thinking that they are talking to their loved one. They have crossed the threshold of actually connecting and experiencing that "aha" moment that it's really happening.

Kevin was faith-filled. He had no fear of death and didn't question that Jocelyn and he would be reunited on the other side. I went to sleep that night in awe of how powerful love and God are. It had been a divine gift for me to witness this living demonstration of God's grace in action. I said prayers of thanksgiving that Kevin was waking up and gratitude for the power of love. Come what may, coma or death, love always finds a way to reach out and connect us.

CHAPTER 19

How's This Possible?

Catherine

After reading the writing, you may find yourself asking how this kind of connection and experience could be possible. To tell the truth, for a long time this same question plagued me. However, over the years I've witnessed hundreds if not thousands of similar experiences. Though each writing is unique, the constant throughout them is a sense of awe and wonder. I've arrived at a place of acceptance and deep gratitude. Sharing my gift today is as natural and normal as any other aspect of my daily life.

This wasn't always the case. When I first started experiencing what might be labeled "extrasensory" interactions, I was bewildered. I didn't really believe they were what they appeared to be. Even less did I understand what was happening. At moments I actually questioned my sanity.

Like everyone, my life has been filled with both challenges and blessings. How many times have I taken an action thinking it was for a particular purpose, only to discover that an unseen hand was guiding me with a quite different objective in mind.

Such incidents can lead to powerful intersections with people, places, and events that only in hindsight do we recognize bear the fingerprints of the hand of destiny.

One pivotal example was my decision in 1985 to quit my job and move to the West Coast. After years of working full time, I had finally saved enough money to be self-supporting and pay cash to finish my education. My scrubby Dutch Aunt Dorothy warned, "People are weird in California. Are you sure you want to move there? Strange things happen there. It's not like here in St. Louis." Old Aunt Dorothy, with her 1960s cat eyeglasses and orthopedic shoes, was the salt of the earth. She had no idea how prophetic her caution would prove to be or that it would soon relate to me directly. Things did become weird, with all the psychic phenomena, and I turned out to be at ground zero for all the mystifying happenings.

Like a lot of "spiritual" gifts, mine came to me unexpectedly. In 1989, when I was 29 and in a graduate program studying communication, I began experiencing unusual and definitely unexplainable occurrences. It all began quite innocently. I was having dinner with a college friend and her sister Kristine who were housesitting for their parents. We were bored, so Kristine suggested we fashion a makeshift Ouija board and play. Those of you who were around in the early 70s remember the Ouija board. Players placed their index fingers lightly on a special indicator piece which moved around a lettered board. Supposedly a spirit gave the participants messages. Of course, it was really someone spelling something out like "Yes, he does like you" or "You'll get your wish."

Kristine got out a yellow legal pad, cut out 26 rectangles, and wrote the alphabet on them. Carefully arranging the letters on her mother's square occasional table, she set a small juice glass in the center. Somehow the lightheartedness felt familiar, like a teenage slumber party—although I don't recall playing the Ouija board back then. It was all in good fun.

The three of us sat around the table, with our index fingers on the downturned glass. At first nothing happened. But when we asked questions, the glass moved hesitantly and roughly, heading slowly to one letter at a time. There was nothing remarkable about that evening, since each of us was certain one of the others was pushing the glass.

A few days later my friend's brother came over and, bored again, we jokingly asked, "Would you like to see our new game?" This time the glass moved more easily, sometimes so rapidly that we had to write down the letters. At the end of the game, we figured out what had been spelled. We then asked, "Who's answering these questions?" The glass moved purposefully to the letters N-O-N-A-M-E. This further intrigued us.

A few days later I told Pam, a fellow graduate student, about these weird events. "I'd like to see it," she enthused. We were trained in good research methodology and taught to trust only empirical evidence. This was a great diversion from the rigors and stress of our graduate program. It was just a game after all.

One afternoon Pam came over to my friend's parents' house to play the Ouija board with us. She was amazed. When the strings of letters were broken into words and read back, they no longer formed just words but complete sentences. Pam keenly pointed out that only when my finger was on the glass did it move with lightning speed.

Exasperated by the one-letter-at-a-time recording and decoding process, Pam asked for a pad of paper and a pen. Once in hand, she thrust them toward me and said, "Obviously it's coming through you, so just write it down." I didn't believe it, but she insisted. So began my ability to be inspired and write down messages whose contents I could have no way of knowing. Though I didn't realize it at the time, I was beginning to receive what has been one of the greatest gifts of my life.

CHAPTER 20

OTHERWORLDLY AND UNEXPLAINABLE THINGS

Catherine

Following the Ouija board experiences, other inexplicable things started to happen, some of them profound. The first oddity involved Kristine. I made an innocent comment about something that triggered her memory of a childhood trauma, and she began crying uncontrollably. As I held her hands trying to comfort her, in my mind's eye I saw in vivid detail a funeral. The focal point was a small white casket near a church altar.

The scene I described had actually taken place, Kristine confirmed. It was the funeral of her baby brother John, an event that had occurred 30 years earlier, when she was only twelve. Even though the memory was depicted in her mind, I was witnessing it in my mind. It was as if I was seeing it through her eyes. A few days after this experience, Kristine told me a stomach issue she had her whole life was now gone.

Kristine told her mom Dolores about the Ouija board incidents and my vision of baby John's funeral. I was surprised when

Dolores thanked me for helping Kristine. *Thank me for what?* I asked myself. *What did I do to help Kristine?*

What happened with Kristine was just the beginning of a long line of otherworldly experiences. I found myself inspired to convey cryptic comments to complete strangers in restaurants and other public places. These were often innocuous and seemingly nonsensical statements, sometimes involving only a few words such as, "The blue truck under the bed."

I had no desire to approach strangers and be seen as crazy, but the directive pounded in my head like a kid pulling at your sleeve, "Say it! Say it! Say it!" Irritated and bewildered, I reluctantly acquiesced.

I would approach the person and say, "Excuse me, I know this is going to sound crazy, but I just want to relay a message to you." Fortunately my appearance was unremarkable, which meant people were neither threatened nor offended. To the contrary, they were generally open and welcoming. Then I'd blurt out the message and say, "Okay, bye." So fast was my exodus that I nearly broke into a run to escape looking more stupid than I already felt.

The oddest things happened. When I delivered a message, the person generally knowingly nodded their head. Sometimes they began to cry or manifest some other form of emotional release. Their reactions and apparent understanding only confused me further. Whoever was with them also looked astonished, as they too struggled to comprehend the person's reaction. Sometimes people called after me, "Wait! Come back. Tell me more." Or they might say, "How did you know that?"

This continued to happen with some regularity, though I couldn't identify a discernible pattern. I really thought I might be losing my mind. But if that were the case, how on earth was I arranging for perfect strangers to collude with me in my insanity?

I quite simply was adrift, confused and fearful that I was losing my grip on reality. In every other way I was a normal person, even excelling in my graduate program. If I was mentally and emotionally losing it, how was I able to function so well and be so high achieving?

As these incidents with strangers continued, my fear, insecurity, and uncertainty escalated. Since Kristine's mom Dolores was, and continues to be, one of the most faith-filled women I know, I turned to her for guidance and support. "Catherine, you have been given the gift of healing," she said matter-of-factly.

What the heck was that, and what did it mean? I wasn't looking for a gift. I was in the middle of a rigorous graduate program. When I signed up for an advanced degree in communication, I didn't mean spirits compelling me to convey unsolicited messages to complete strangers.

Dolores tried to convince me that this gift was a blessing, but I wasn't buying it. Instead, I was worried. Wasn't this Ouija board stuff the "devil's work"? Had I unwittingly let in a dark force?

When I remained unconvinced, Dolores arranged for me to meet two of her friends, both of whom were not only priests but also practicing psychologists. Pouring out my heart, with all my confusion and fear, I was surprised to find they weren't shocked. Instead they asked questions such as, "How did people respond when you approached them? Were they frightened or upset?"

I explained, "No. Unbelievably, they recognized the significance of the message, usually accompanied by an emotional reaction. They even expressed gratitude."

The priests told me that although this was indeed unusual and they empathized with my concern, what I was describing was actually a gift from God—specifically, something classed as a "gift of the Spirit." They showed me Bible passages that spoke of gifts similar to what I was experiencing.

I needed more assurance that there was nothing evil involved in what was transpiring. The priests told me, "Judge these gifts by their fruits. If they help people, you know they are from God.

But if you see any ill effects, then the origin could be darker and you should stop doing it."

My concern was that I couldn't prevent these messages from coming even if I tried. I didn't seek them out and I couldn't stop them. They were spontaneous, all encompassing, and not within my ability to control. These and other experiences continued to occur, compelling me to question and ultimately transcend my beliefs about miracles, mysteries, and even what I knew about reality.

CHAPTER 21

GOD WRITINGS

Catherine

In the years that followed, my otherworldly experiences continued to evolve. The source that initially described itself as "No Name" shortly after we had those few and only Ouija board games now identified itself as "God."

The unpredictable, uncontrollable urge to convey messages to strangers waned with time, and I learned that I could modulate them. The "God writings," as I came to call them, always began with the words, "God. Welcome." When the session drew to a close, it simply closed, "Go With God."

A pen and paper, together with my willingness to help others, were my only necessary tools. The short messages became inspirations of full dialogues in prose, with rich and moving imagery, relevant and significant to the particular recipient. Through this gift, God continued to offer intimate and profound wisdom and guidance, which supported people's growth and healing. Unique metaphors specific to each individual addressed their deeper issues, often without them ever asking a question. The divine knew exactly what they needed to hear.

The God writings are always insightful. The guidance covers a full spectrum of human experiences, including behavior, relationships, decision-making, and self-growth. Using clarifying images and metaphors, frequently the source or root of a behavior or belief that no longer serves the person is identified. Once the mechanisms that keep these patterns or beliefs in place are revealed, the person can choose to liberate themselves from them. The wisdom also sometimes comes as suggestions, at other times as direction, always lovingly and gently offered. These writings speak to each person in their own vernacular, articulated uniquely for the recipient's way of thinking and understanding. The consistent quality in all of the God writings is an abiding love that's attuned and responsive to each person's deeper yearnings, fears, and needs. The focus is always to liberate recipients from whatever may be blocking them, including their limitations, outmoded self-perceptions, or behavior patterns that no longer serve them.

I don't recall the first instance when the writings expanded to include inspirations that facilitated connections with deceased people, but it was probably within three months from when the gift began. Sometimes during a God writing, I feel the deceased person's energy and am inspired to connect them with their loved ones.

Like the Kevin and Jocelyn writings, these are not generic "I miss you" messages. They are full dialogues about issues, people, and events known only by the person for whom I'm writing. These interactions bring people comfort, resolution, and closure. The rich details I write are usually spot-on, and they are always filled with loving intent that impacts both the recipients and myself.

Whether it's God's or a deceased person's inspiration, almost everyone receiving a writing is amazed at the specificity of the information shared. It isn't uncommon for them to stare at me with their mouths open as if I'd gone through their underwear drawer, imagining that I must know absolutely all of their deepest secrets. It isn't true, of course. I know very little to nothing about them or their lives.

I don't know why or how I am the recipient of this gift. I believe we all have gifts, none of them less or more important than others. For me this gift comes with a responsibility to share it with the same light and love from which it's derived. Through almost three decades of experience, I maintain the same level of reverence and awe each time I do a writing. My encounters have increased my appreciation and understanding of love, consciousness, the nature of reality, and God. My relationship with God and my understanding of myself continue to evolve, expand, and grow. I am continually moved by the insight I receive and the connection I experience from my work with people.

The God writings in this book are the actual ones I shared with Jocelyn in real time. Though they are personal and specific to Kevin and Jocelyn, they offer all of us an opportunity to explore what they mean to us in the context of our own lives and experiences.

CHAPTER 22

TAP MY FINGERS

Catherine

About ten days after the first writing with Jocelyn, I was back from vacation and her sister Vicky and I got together. She took my arm, hugged me, and thanked me for what I had done for Kevin and Jocelyn.

"I've got to show you what Kevin did," she enthused.

"I know," I said. "It's amazing. You tapped his fingers and he woke up."

She said, "No. I have to show you what he did. Give me your hand."

I said, "I know he tapped your fingers back."

She was insistent, "Give me your hand. I want to show you."

I thought it was odd for Vicky to be so persistent, so I agreed and reached out my hand as if to shake hers.

"No, not like that," she instructed, placing my hand under hers, with her hand resting on top of mine. Then she did the most extraordinary thing. Using her index and middle fingers she began to rapidly tap her fingers on the top of my hand. In that moment, chills went through me.

To be sure I had understood, I said, "You tapped his fingers first, right?"

She said, "No, I didn't. He tapped my hand with his fingers."

I felt all the tumblers in my brain turn. What was she saying—that he tapped her hand first?

During the writing on the phone, Kevin had the idea to do an experiment to tap his fingers and see if he could tap back. Jocelyn had asked Vicky to tap Kevin's fingers. Kevin was communicating with me, Jocelyn was talking, and I could hear Vicky on the speakerphone. It was all happening at once, so it was a bit confusing.

Jocelyn said to Vicky, "Kevin wants you to tap his fingers."

Vicky asked why, and Jocelyn said, "Just do it."

Vicky replied, "He's taking my hand. He's squeezing my hand."

Simultaneously I felt Kevin's energy communicate, "I'm doing it." Even though we were a thousand miles away, Jocelyn, Vicky, and I were all extremely excited. It was amazing enough that Kevin had managed to rouse himself. But that he initiated the tapping experiment blew my mind.

Vicky provided the following detailed account of exactly what happened in Kevin's hospital room that night:

> As always, Kevin neither reacted to me nor looked at me when I arrived. Several nurses came in and prepared him for bed. He was poker-faced, and it was impossible to tell whether he was awake or asleep. I turned on the TV to watch the last episode of *The Bachelor*. The volume was so low that I could barely hear it and the room was dark. My phone rang and Jocelyn said, "Kevin wants to do an experiment."
>
> I turned the TV off and walked around to the other side of the bed to turn on the lights. My back was to Kevin as I was turning them on. As Jocelyn said, "We want you to …" I turned around and was startled to see that Kevin's arm, which had been resting on the bed,

was now reaching out to me. He raised his right arm, extending his hand! I quickly extended my right hand out to his and he grabbed it just as Jocelyn finished her sentence "… hold Kevin's hand."

I told Jocelyn, "He was already reaching for me when I turned around and he is holding it now!"

"What?" Jocelyn exclaimed.

"He's already holding my hand!"

I could hear you two [Catherine and Jocelyn] talking in the background, but I was focused on Kevin and wasn't sure what you were saying. His grip over the top of my hand was firm. Then he started tapping the top of my hand with his index finger. I said, "He's now tapping my hand with his index finger."

Then I heard you [Catherine] say, "Wow, it's really working." I didn't know what precipitated this at all, whose idea this was, or how this hand tapping defined what was "working."

Kevin tapped for a while and I could hear you and Jocelyn talking on the phone about how amazed you were that he was doing this. All I knew was that Kevin somehow knew I was there, and that he had a firm grip on my hand. I was focused on his hand and trying to tell you both what was happening. But when I finally looked at his face, his eyes were very intensely open and alert, and I had not seen them like that before. I was amazed that he was doing something that he was obviously conscious about doing.

Jocelyn said she would be back to Kevin's hospital room soon. I stood there holding Kevin's gripping hand. The tapping had stopped, and I stayed like that until he decided to let go of my hand. I hoped he would stay this way until Jocelyn came back, and he stayed like that for at least fifteen minutes.

Kevin was always such a gentleman. Right before he let go of my hand, he did something that was so sweet and moving that I will never forget it. He lifted my hand to his face and kissed the back of my hand, then gently released it. I was touched beyond words. I know this was his way of saying, "Thank you, Vicky." Every time I think about that moment, it touches my heart deeply.

As Vicky recounted what Kevin had done, I realized the truth. Kevin hadn't simply conducted an experiment to tap his fingers. It wasn't as I had envisioned the experiment. It didn't entail asking someone to tap his fingers to give him sensory input. His experiment was far more ingenious. His real experiment was to verify whether his brain, in a dream state or not, could send a message and command his body to tap his own fingers. When he executed it, he was able to raise his state of awareness. It's possible that this alone had a greater impact than the medical procedures he had undergone.

A few of my previous writings had involved comatose patients who also thought they were merely dreaming. So Kevin's situation wasn't the first I'd come across. As with Kevin, comatose patients' internal or conscious experiences were far more active and alive than we traditionally believe. Although these communications were comforting and healing to their loved ones, sadly they didn't wake up.

This experience with Kevin further confirmed for me that the boundaries of our consciousness aren't as fixed as we've been taught to believe. I think there is something more here that should be studied and explored. When our intentions and consciousness are coupled with divine energy and presence, maybe we can create miracles in our lives and in the lives of others.

CHAPTER 23

A State of Being

Jocelyn

People often say that marriage is hard work, or that they had to work hard to be happily married. I never understood that. It's like saying you have to work hard at having fun. If I had to work hard at being happily married, I wouldn't have been. Either you are happy in your marriage or you are not. It's a state of being, not a job.

Kevin and I were more than happily married. From the day we met until long after he died, we were crazy about each other. Of course, we annoyed the crap out of each other sometimes, but it was never over something serious. We had the usual problems of any married couple with children—struggles with finances in the early years, the ups and downs of raising kids, work pressures, family problems, and all the other curveballs that life throws at you in the course of living it. But between the two of us, it was always great.

People tell me now what a blessing it was that we were so happy, and how lucky I am to have had that kind of relationship. I am. I know that. I also know that most people aren't still crazy in love with their spouses after almost 25 years of marriage like we were. It would have been much easier to cope with his illness and then his death if Kevin had been an inconsiderate asshole who I barely tolerated in a loveless marriage.

I met Kevin when I worked in his law firm one summer while I was in law school. He was 33 and a partner, whereas I was a 25-year-old intern. We were both smitten from the get-go. He had just ended his first marriage and wasn't looking for another relationship. I had one more year in law school and was planning to practice in another country. After spending an evening with Kevin in the Chinese restaurant and then the parking lot at his office, I went home and told my mother I had met the man I was going to marry. No wonder I've always been a sucker for romance novels.

Kevin and I were really different from each other. He was a proper and upright man. He liked rules and followed them when they didn't even make sense. I always felt that rules were more like guidelines you could ignore if you weren't going to get caught. If we were driving somewhere in the middle of the night and came to a stoplight with nobody around for miles, he sat there for what seemed an eternity waiting for the light to change. Kevin liked order in his life and to plan things out. He thought about his words carefully before he spoke them. I am a spur-of-the-moment kind of person with no filter. I say whatever pops into my head. He was always reading a spiritual book or something with meaning like a biography, and I like mindless novels that require no thinking at all. He loved politics and world affairs and wanted to understand the world around him. I like celebrity gossip and don't see the value in filling my mind with history and meaningful topics. He always dressed nicely, whereas I opted for comfort, which often meant sweats and slippers that I wore even when out.

Despite our many surface differences, at our core we had the same values. We were both fiercely loyal to friends and family, both had a strong work ethic, both felt intensely about inequality and discrimination in all forms, and we laughed all the time.

Our differences made for a fun relationship. We bantered back and forth constantly. We joked, chided, and teased each other over our silly differences, all of which we found endearing in each other. We were super affectionate and were always touching each other—holding hands when we walked, cuddling on the couch while watching TV, and exchanging little kisses in the grocery store. Even after 25 years together, we held hands across the dinner table when we were eating out. It was just such a natural extension of our connection. I can't really think of a time when we were in touching distance and weren't doing so.

CHAPTER 24

A FLOWER ON MY PILLOW

Jocelyn

Kevin was a much better person than I am in all ways. He still is. I always knew I got the better end of the deal in our relationship. I kept waiting for him to figure out that I wasn't worthy of him. He treasured me, and I honestly couldn't understand why. He did little things every day to show me how he felt about me.

I always got up first. Every morning, even if he was running late, he made the bed. Then he went outside, picked a flower, and put it on my pillow. If he had to leave for work before I got up, I'd find a flower under my windshield wiper. He always took a shower first. When he was done, he placed a fresh towel next to the shower for me so I wouldn't have to get one. Little daily things like these seemed small and insignificant at the time, but they let me know how much Kevin treasured me and wanted me to know it. He was the most thoughtful person I ever knew. When he became sick, he wasn't worried for himself, wasn't worried about dying. He was worried about the kids and me.

Kevin was very religious, but not in a Bible-thumping, fundamentalist way. His was a quiet belief, well thought out and considered. He had such a strong faith about what was next for him. I don't know how other people face dying, but with Kevin he really wasn't concerned about it at all for himself. I, on the other hand, was scared shitless about him dying. I felt selfish because I didn't want him to go. I was mad at God and the universe for taking him away from me and everyone else who loved him. When we knew he only had months left, Kevin still always thought of me and our children first. He still put a flower on my pillow every morning until the day we went to UCLA for his surgery.

After this writing with Catherine, I realized that nothing had changed between us. Kevin was still a much finer person than I thought I could ever be. He was still putting his family first. He still loved me, even though he couldn't express it in the ways he did before. After the writing was over, I once again thought I was the luckiest woman on earth to be his wife and still didn't understand what I ever did to deserve him.

CHAPTER 25

WAKING UP

Jocelyn

In the days following Catherine's writing, Kevin started to wake up. It wasn't like he just sat up the next day as if nothing had happened and asked me for a cup of coffee. Nor was I expecting this, since it wasn't within the realm of possibility given that he had undergone five brain surgeries in 26 days, together with several additional invasive procedures. There were three surgeries on July 10 alone: the first to remove Kevin's brain tumor, the second to repair a ruptured artery, and the third to insert a tube into his ventricles.

Next came a surgery to insert a shunt to drain the fluid from Kevin's brain down into his body, a procedure that also required insertion of a permanent magnetic device in his forehead to control the amount of fluid draining from his brain. A final surgery followed to equalize the fluid between his two ventricles. Kevin had also been subjected to a spinal tap because he had nerve damage to his face and the doctors thought that his cancer may have spread to his spinal cord. Since he was constantly loaded up with pain medication, there was no way even under the best of circumstances that Kevin could fully wake up and be like he was before all this happened.

Despite this, he did become much more alert and responsive, whereas he really wasn't before Catherine's writing. In that sense his condition was like night and day. He went from being comatose to being able to communicate in small ways. He could give a thumb's up or a thumb's down when asked questions by the doctors. He could move one leg or the other when requested to do so. He also started to talk a little. It wasn't a miraculous transformation, given that he still had a long way to go before he could engage in meaningful interactions, but it was a huge turnaround from where he had been. With things finally starting to look up, I was more hopeful than I had been in weeks.

CHAPTER 26

OUR 24ᵀᴴ ANNIVERSARY

Jocelyn

Kevin's most coherent and alert day up to this point was on August 12, 2013, the date of our 24ᵗʰ wedding anniversary. Exactly one week had passed since the first writing with Catherine.

Kevin and I always celebrated our anniversary. If we were in Santa Barbara, we went back to San Ysidro Ranch, where we got married in the ranch's garden. We stood under the same arbor where we had exchanged our vows, held hands, and told each other how much we loved each other. I realize it sounds sappy, and it was. As I mentioned earlier, Kevin was a sentimental guy and loved these kinds of dorky but sweet traditions.

On our 20ᵗʰ wedding anniversary, we were in Bass Lake for our annual summer trip with our neighbors. I planned a surprise recommitment ceremony for us. We both were so happy. Twenty years is a milestone in any marriage, deserving of a celebration. That we were so many years in and still so smitten with each other was practically unheard of. Since this was before he became sick, I remember thinking at the time that I would plan a repeat when we hit our 25ᵗʰ anniversary.

When we were in the hospital on our 24th anniversary, I found myself thinking about that recommitment ceremony. Would we make it to our 25th? Just as I was mulling the prospect over, a nurse entered the room. When I shared with her that it was our anniversary, she asked Kevin how long we had been married. The nurses always talked to Kevin like he would respond, even though he never did. Now, however, he surprised us both. "Not long enough," he replied. Hearing him reply was the best anniversary gift I had ever received from him—and he was big on gift giving.

It's funny how, when you are in a situation that's beyond terrible, a little less terrible seems like the greatest gift. That's how it was for me. I understood that Kevin would never be the same as he was before the surgery. I realized he was still going to die from brain cancer in a year or less. But I was now hopeful that in the time we had left, he would recover to the point we could enjoy meaningful time together.

A few days prior to our anniversary, I received two jokes by email from a friend. One concerned a billboard that read, "Need Help? Call 1 (555) I GOT GOD." Under the circumstances this didn't seem all that funny. The other joke was culturally insensitive, yet I found it funny. It was about a man who was having a really rough time in his life. At the point when he was all out of hope, he saw a sign by the side of the road that read "Need help? Call Jesus," with a phone number below it. The man called the number, and the next day a Hispanic gardener showed up.

Since this second joke injected a little lightheartedness into our bleak situation, I emailed it to Catherine and several friends. Catherine called me after she received the email. Because the nurse was in the hospital room changing Kevin's sheets at the time, I stepped into the hallway to take the call. Catherine and I had been in contact by text and a few phone calls since the August 5 writing, since she wanted to know whether Kevin was doing any better. She was as excited as I was that he had started to wake up.

When I returned to the room, Kevin and I engaged in the most coherent interaction we had experienced since his surgery. He said, "He's pulling for you Jocelyn." I was shocked that he said such a complete thought in a single sentence.

I asked, "Who, Kevin?"

"Jesus," he replied. It was beyond weird—truly freaky. I hadn't read the email joke to him, and he had no way of knowing that I had forwarded it to Catherine or that I had just spoken to her. He just said it out of the blue.

Kevin and I often knew what the other was thinking. It was something we both thought unusual, and we chalked it up to just being really in sync with each other. We used to laugh when one of us said something and the other replied, "How did you know I was just thinking about that?"

Kevin's comment about Jesus seemed so much more unusual than just a husband and wife knowing each other so well that they often knew what the other was thinking. Besides, given the circumstances, I wasn't thinking that any higher power loved me. If there was a loving God, why was Kevin so sick?

CHAPTER 27

1 (555) I GOT GOD

Catherine

Prior to the first writing, Kevin had been unresponsive for weeks. Kevin tapped his fingers and roused himself at that precise moment when we were on the phone having a session. Most people dismiss coincidences, but I have learned from experience—my own and that of others—that signs and even divine synchronicities happen all the time. These statistically improbable occurrences are too precise and timely to be random. For Kevin to speak to Jocelyn on their anniversary was just such an occurrence.

At times we have all experienced strange events we might call "intuition." Kevin wasn't only responding coherently, which was unbelievable in itself, but he was also responding to the specific content of a joke of which he had no awareness. The timing of his statement was uncanny. Despite calendars and sophisticated minds, it's common for people to forget anniversaries. So how was Kevin able to speak so coherently on this particular day, their wedding anniversary? Especially in view of the fact that he had endured five brain surgeries in the space of five weeks.

The reason that comes to my mind is love.

Love is more powerful than illness, more powerful than any-thing that would limit us. Like a woman who can muster the strength to lift a car off her child pinned beneath it, Kevin had defied all limitations. Not only was he speaking more coherently for the first time since his last surgery, he also seemed to be aware of Jocelyn's email. He found a way to give her the most meaning-ful present, a sign that he was there and aware.

I see these events through a spiritual lens, and consequently I am always in awe. Universal love, Source, God, or Creator—whatever name you give it—is so good. It struck me that Kevin didn't say, "Happy anniversary, I love you." He said, "You know he's pulling for you, Jocelyn." When she asked who he meant, he answered "Jesus." How did he know about that email? Was he able to leave his body? Or was it, as Jocelyn said, that they always knew what the other was thinking? Maybe it wasn't just a random coincidence, but a sign or a divine synchronicity.

How many times have you had a direct experience of "know-ing," or felt guided or directed by something outside your own volition? Have you, or someone you know, had something seemingly random happen that resulted in your or their whole life taking a different trajectory?

Sure, it's easy to dismiss such occurrences as mere coinci-dences. They don't tidily fit into our logical understanding of reality. Can you think of any significant so-called coincidences you have experienced that led you to avert a problem? Have you ever followed a hunch that saved you from danger or perhaps even disaster? We hear these kinds of stories frequently. A traveler is delayed or took a different route and avoided an accident as a result.

Our intuition can also facilitate positive events or outcomes. It seems wise to pay attention and listen to our intuition or gut feelings. By intuition or gut feelings, I'm referring to those ideas, inner guidance or directions, imbued with strong feeling, energy, or senses that transcend our usual intellectual or rational bases for knowing alone.

We have all heard about odd and improbable accounts of chance meetings, lucky breaks, and other events that seemingly involve the divine. With my gift, these synchronicities are normal and common. I hope you pause the next time a "coincidence" comes your way and that you ask yourself whether it could be a sign, synchronicity, or a divine manifestation.

In my writings and in my life I'm continually invited to witness firsthand the transcendent blessings that are beyond what we can imagine. There is always an open window for grace and God's blessings to pour into our lives, even if others believe it's just a coincidence. I much prefer to call these kinds of things signs or divine synchronicities.

"Need help? Call 1 (555) I GOT GOD." This is neither wishful thinking nor an act of desperation. To the contrary, it's a recognition that this all-loving Source is always present in our lives. Though we may not receive all we desire or a full healing, God comes to us, lifts us up, holds us, and tends us in the most exquisite ways.

Jocelyn didn't share Kevin's belief and devotion. Instead, she was angry and railing against this so-called all powerful and loving God who was putting her and her family through so much pain. Kevin's anniversary present to Jocelyn that night wasn't just encouragement that he was waking up. It was prophetic in a sense. He wanted to remind her of Jesus as a source and resource of support. Regardless of our particular belief system, it's a reminder to us that the universe holds mysteries which we cannot explain, despite all of our advanced yet infinitesimal understandings. But they are nevertheless real.

We are created by and for love. Help and connection are always one breath, one prayer, one realization, or one awakening away.

CHAPTER 28

REHABILITATION

Jocelyn

During that first writing after I asked Kevin what he wanted me to do going forward, I had some difficult decisions to make given his condition. I tried to get him admitted into a rehabilitation facility in Santa Barbara, which he said he wanted, but they wouldn't take him. UCLA had evaluated him before the first writing and didn't want to take him either. Since he wasn't awake, they said Kevin wouldn't benefit from rehab.

The rehabilitation staff at UCLA reevaluated him once he started to wake up after the writing. They still said he wasn't sufficiently alert to benefit from therapy even though he was definitely more awake. He required around-the-clock nursing care, was receiving daily breathing treatments for pneumonia, and still had both a trach tube and a feeding tube. UCLA wanted me to send Kevin to a skilled nursing facility, but I refused. I knew that if he went into a place like that, he would never come out.

In a last ditch effort, I met with the head of the UCLA rehabilitation facility and begged him to give Kevin a chance. It seemed to me that, given he was waking up more and more each day, therapy could help him. I told them that if UCLA's rehabilitation facility wasn't an option, then I would take Kevin home, care for him myself, hire nurses to help me, and pay for private rehabilitation therapy.

Part of what an acute rehabilitation facility does is teach the family members how to take care of the person on their own. If the rehabilitation facility insisted that Kevin wouldn't benefit from rehabilitation, someone needed to teach me how to take care of him myself. For example, I needed to be able to get Kevin from his bed to a wheelchair, then in and out of the shower without dropping him.

Kevin was 6'2" and I'm 5'4." It's really hard to safely move someone ten inches taller than you from a bed to a wheelchair, then to a shower and back. I also needed to learn how to change the linens on his hospital bed with Kevin in it, and how to use the feeding tube and clean and change his trach tube. He still couldn't sit up on his own, or even hold his head up without support.

While the UCLA doctors weren't especially hopeful about the amount of progress Kevin would make in two weeks, they changed their minds and agreed to admit Kevin into their program. He was moved to the UCLA rehabilitation unit on August 15. The first few days were hopeful. Even the rehabilitation staff were surprised how well he was functioning. When the speech therapist came in, Kevin was able to answer questions about how many children he had, where he lived, his favorite musicians and foods, and so on. They were only one or two-word answers, but Kevin could formulate the correct responses.

The staff put Kevin on a reclining bike and strapped his feet into the pedals. For the first few minutes, they had the pedals turn automatically. When they turned this feature off, Kevin kept peddling. After a few days they even took out his trach tube in an attempt to teach Kevin how to swallow again, which unfortunately he couldn't. Despite this, things were definitely looking up and I had real hope that he was on the road to recovery. Kevin seemed to be able to focus on and recognize the person talking to him. While in a sitting position, Kevin was also able to hold his head up without support.

For the first time since everything had gone wrong following that second brain surgery, I had visions of Kevin being back at home, sitting on our deck enjoying the warm weather and being able to talk a little back and forth. Even if it was just for a few months, I wanted to have even a fraction of the connection we enjoyed before. I knew that Kevin would never be back to the way he was prior to the surgery, but I really thought we were going to have some quality time together before his cancer came back again and he died.

It's funny how one's expectations change so much in such a short time. When Kevin first went in for the second brain surgery on July 10, 2013, I imagined we would be home in four days. I anticipated that he would be fully functioning, just like he was after the first surgery three and a half years earlier. I knew his time would be limited, but I thought we would get to enjoy that time together. We were going to make our last year count for all the years that we weren't going to have together.

We planned to travel to Israel and see the Holy Land, since this was one of Kevin's lifelong dreams. He also planned on spending what time remained with the people who had been important to him during his life, but who he hadn't seen in recent years. We were going to have one last family summer trip to Bass Lake.

Fast-forward to the end of August. All I was hoping for now was maybe a few months to just sit quietly in our home and appreciate each other for whatever time Kevin had left.

CHAPTER 29

PRACTICALLY COMATOSE

Jocelyn

After less than a week in rehabilitation, Kevin began to go downhill again, this time rapidly. He stopped responding to commands to hold up one finger or two, wasn't able to answer any questions, and had no control over his body. He just lay in bed, with his one good eye open, though, we suspected, not seeing anything. He couldn't hold his head up, and if you tried to prop him up, he fell like a brick to one side. Obviously he could no longer participate in any of the rehabilitation exercises. Within ten days of starting therapy, Kevin was basically back to how he had been before the first writing—comatose.

During Kevin's second and final week in rehabilitation, I made arrangements to take him home. There was nothing more that could be done for Kevin by either the rehabilitation facility or the hospital now that he was once again comatose. In terms of any treatment, we were at the end of the line. Either I was going to have to send Kevin to a skilled nursing facility or take him home.

Since there was no way I was going to place Kevin in a skilled nursing facility, he was going home. Everything I needed to take care of him had been ordered—a hospital bed, a wheelchair, a bathing chair for the shower, medical supplies, among other items. My sister had cleared out our bedroom so that everything could be set up. Medical care had been arranged through our local Visiting Nurses Association. I had lined up private duty help and a neurological rehabilitation specialist.

The reality was that I was excited we would soon be going home. We had been at UCLA since July 10 and it was now August 28, 2013. Like most people, I hate hospitals, and I'd been living in one for the last seven weeks.

CHAPTER 30

FINALLY GOING HOME

Jocelyn

Kevin had more than a dozen CT scans during the course of his last seven weeks. The hospital had administered an MRI almost a month before, which didn't show any new tumor growth. I asked the oncologist to order one more MRI before we went home, to which he agreed. So on the day before we left rehab, Kevin had one more MRI.

I was beyond relieved that this phase was coming to a close. The ambulance was due the following morning at 10:00 a.m. We were finally going home.

I had thought a lot over the last few weeks about the writing I experienced with Catherine, during the time Kevin was in a coma at the beginning of the month. How could I not think about it? If I hadn't actually had the experience, I wouldn't have believed it. I'd told a few of my closest friends about it, but they didn't believe it was true or even possible. I for one had no doubts about what I had experienced, and I knew that I had communicated with Kevin during that writing, even though he was in a coma. Not only was I able to get his thoughts on what we should do next in terms of his treatment, I was able to tell him he wasn't dreaming. He was able to wake himself up more after that.

Catherine offered to do another writing after we were back in Santa Barbara, and I was totally on board with that. Since Kevin couldn't communicate with me in the traditional way, I was thrilled that I was going to talk with him again.

I hadn't been home even once since the second brain surgery. I thought that if Kevin was home, he could really get the rest he needed to recover to the point where we could engage in some meaningful interaction again. Even though he had declined a lot in the last week, I attributed it to him just being exhausted and needing some real peace and quiet. I was sure he missed our home just as much as I did. There was nothing left to do except get there, and I was thinking that in 24 hours we would finally be home.

CHAPTER 31

IT'S IMPORTANT THAT I COME TODAY

Catherine

ocelyn and I had talked about doing another writing once Kevin returned to Santa Barbara. On the day before Kevin was due home, I woke up with a strong sense that I should do an in-person writing right away, even before they returned to Santa Barbara. To be respectful and not intrusive, I tried to ignore the strong sense I had that the writing couldn't wait.

When the urge to go persisted, I asked Vicky if she would drive me since I was recovering from surgery to repair a detached retina and couldn't yet drive myself. Los Angeles traffic can be horrendous, so I had to reschedule other commitments. When my schedule cleared with ease, I took it as a sign that I had made the right decision.

Only then did I call Jocelyn to ask if I could come. She was resistant and offered lots of protests. "Don't bother—there's no need. And the drive is too long. Besides, we'll be home soon enough. Can't it wait?"

I'm assertive, but not pushy or insensitive. I said, "No, Vicky can bring me and I don't mind at all. I believe it's important that I come today." Reluctantly, Jocelyn agreed we could come.

CHAPTER 32

IT CAN'T WAIT
UNTIL TOMORROW

Jocelyn

When Catherine called me out of the blue and asked to come down to UCLA, I told her that it was unnecessary. She insisted, which I now know is unusual for her, telling me, "It can't wait until tomorrow."

We had kept in touch during the last month, and I had given her regular updates on how Kevin was progressing. She knew his condition had significantly improved following the first writing, but that it was declining again. I was extremely worried that something was seriously wrong. Why else would she insist on coming down to UCLA that day?

It was clear she felt somebody needed to tell me something before we came home. I was fearful that it was something really bad, because if it wasn't, then it could certainly wait a day. Since she was so insistent, I told her to come.

I'd never had a writing with Catherine in person, so I didn't know what to expect. I didn't know whether she fell into some

101

weird trance or perhaps needed complete silence. I didn't know whether incense or candles were involved, which was how I visualized something like that. I didn't know whether she had any control over what was going to unfold.

Basically, all I knew about any of it was what I had experienced when we were over a thousand miles apart. I had only seen Catherine a few times in social settings, so I really didn't know her all that well. Suffice it to say, I was apprehensive for a lot of reasons when she showed up at UCLA.

Catherine met me in Kevin's hospital room, and I could tell from the expression on her face when she first saw him how shocked she was by his appearance and condition. His jaw was slack, his skinny body limp. He looked nothing like the vibrant and handsome man he was before the surgery. I was used to how he looked now because I watched the transition as it occurred. I moved Kevin from his bed to the wheelchair and we all went outside to the hospital patio.

Once we were all seated, Catherine took out several writing pens and a clipboard with paper. She seemed relaxed and friendly, like she was having a cup of coffee with a friend. That was it—no candles, no incense, no trance-like state. I didn't know what I was expecting, but it wasn't this.

CHAPTER 33

A BLIND EYE

Catherine

When Vicky and I arrived at UCLA, Kevin was motionless in his hospital bed. One eye was wide open, staring blankly, the other stitched shut. I was shocked by Kevin's physical condition. Knowing that Jocelyn planned to bring him home the next day, I hadn't expected him to appear so incapacitated.

Jocelyn thanked us for coming and reiterated how unnecessary it was because they were going home. She wanted all of us, including Kevin, to go outside for more privacy to do the writing. Seeing Kevin's condition, I couldn't imagine it would be possible.

Jocelyn told us she had been training for days to master all the aspects of Kevin's care. She positioned the wheelchair, lowered the bed, sat Kevin up despite the fact he was dead weight, and proceeded to hold him up and put a strap around him. When he began to lean and topple over, the nurse standing next to his bed attempted to help Jocelyn stabilize him, which caused Jocelyn to snap at her, "No! Don't touch him. Don't help me. I'll do it."

I was taken aback by how adamant and abrupt Jocelyn was, as if she were defending herself. As it turned out, she was able to maneuver him, lifting with her knees, using all her might, straining, and grunting with a "1, 2, 3, lift." In one laborious movement, she maneuvered him into the wheelchair. It was painful to witness how strongly she recoiled and rejected the nurse's help. She was Kevin's dragonslayer. She wheeled him to the nurses' station with us in tow.

Kevin had been given an MRI the evening before, and the nurses were stalling on giving Jocelyn the results. She was almost frothing with frustration and anger. The nurses offered the standard disclaimers—not hospital policy, the doctor hasn't reviewed it yet, and so on.

Exasperated, Jocelyn spat out, "We'll see about that. I'll be back, and you better have it by then."

It had been three and a half weeks since Kevin's last MRI, and his condition had recently deteriorated significantly. Jocelyn confided to us that she had a bad feeling the cancer was back.

With Kevin strapped into the wheelchair, we went outside to a large secluded patio area. "Kevin and I come out here all the time," Jocelyn explained. Hugging him and speaking tenderly to him, she continued, "Isn't that right, Kevie? And tomorrow we will be back in our own home."

Kevin displayed no awareness of Jocelyn's presence. On the way to the patio, she talked about all the arrangements she had made for home—the private nurses and the equipment.

"I'm sure he'll be just as glad as me to be home," she told me. "You can't rest in hospitals. All he needs is time to rest and recover." She seemed oblivious of his ever-worsening condition. Sometimes that's what love does—turns a blind eye. Love puts the rose-colored glasses on and endures, eternally optimistic and hopeful.

Vicky had asked me on the drive down, "What do you think will happen? Will God or Kevin show up?"

"I have no idea," I told her, "beyond feeling I need to go now and not wait. Even if nothing comes through, we can still support Jocelyn." Even as I got out my clipboard, pen and paper to do the writing, I had no idea what would be said or why I was there.

Until I actual dip into the energy, receive the inspiration, and write, rarely do I sense the topic, much less whether the energy of the comatose or deceased person will be available. Jocelyn seemed apprehensive, understandably. When I asked her if she wanted to begin, she said, "Yes."

And so the writing began.

SECOND WRITING

August 29, 2013

CHAPTER 34

THE VEIL OPENS

Kevin, Jocelyn and Catherine

JOCELYN: Since I don't know who is going to show up, I have no questions prepared.

When I had the first writing by phone with Catherine, my sister Vicky told me I should have a list of questions prepared so I didn't forget to ask whoever was going to show up those questions to which I wanted answers. As it turned out in the first writing, after Kevin said, "I'm here" and our conversation began, I completely ignored my questions.

CATHERINE: Oh no, it doesn't matter. You don't need any questions. Obviously it works regardless. I mean that's the great thing—it is what it is. We are just in this place of receiving whatever is there. He could be able—he could be unable. You know what I mean? Who knows?

This answered my question about whether she had any control over what happened during the writings. I was surprised

108

that she appeared to be just as clueless as I was about what would happen.

JOCELYN: I'm hoping it's Kevin.

CATHERINE: I don't ever know. That's the whole thing. I always say I have no idea until it happens. I'm as clueless as you are. I just show up and see what happens. Right, Kevin?

JOCELYN: I'd love that kind of gift. Just show up and see who shows up for me.

CATHERINE: It's the only place in my life that I'm not addicted to the product and want it to be perfect. I'm just as amazed as the people I write for. There isn't any place else in my life that I can operate this freely.

JOCELYN: How do you turn it off and on? Do you just go, "Okay, I'm ready?"

CATHERINE: It's always there. It's like a stream of energy I can dip into. I think it's always the case for all of us. For some reason I can just dip in, but I don't think there's anything unique about me, Catherine. I think we are all capable. We simply don't know it or aren't available for it.

JOCELYN: I can clearly tell you that this isn't my skill set. I don't have any "dipping in" capabilities.

CATHERINE: Believe me, nowhere else in my life am I like this.

Catherine began doing the writing.

JOCELYN: Are you going to read it out loud? It's up to you.

CATHERINE: Yeah, sure.

JOCELYN: Whatever you normally do is fine with me.

CATHERINE: "God. Welcome, Jocelyn and Kevin." This is the God part.

JOCELYN: He's saying that?

CATHERINE: No, God always has the introductions.

JOCELYN: Okay.

GOD: "Welcome, Jocelyn and Kevin.

The sweet lace sits down, worn perhaps and tattered in places unseen, but this veil is not as it appears. The division is transparent, for the heart knows no such divisions. The lace is worn thinner now, and the grace of God shines forward, as if the sunlit room is seen. The gentle breeze blows forth a delightfulness that says there is no death, no darkness. The vacancy isn't a reflection of the spirit, which is full of light and vitality. The lace curtains thin—the veil opens."

> *The veil, Kevin's consciousness, was worn and tattered. God clarified that despite the brain's condition, "the heart knows no such divisions." It's possible that the heart, rather than the brain, was aware and could grasp and understand. The vacancy that Kevin exuded wasn't the truth of his state. God's light was in illumination within him. The reference to the lace being thinner and the veil being open could signify that Kevin's consciousness was transitioning from this earthly realm to the heavenly realm.*

> *Since this was the first time I had received a writing in person, I didn't understand the mechanics of how it works. Catherine just starts writing furiously fast, then pauses and reads what she's written. That's just what she did. When she paused to read me the introduction, I couldn't believe that she had written something so poetic, so quickly. When you are sitting with her, it seems impossible that she can write as fast as she does, and it still makes perfect sense.*

KEVIN: I'm not sleeping. I'm here. I'm not dreaming. I see. I'm not alone—you are here with me.

I looked at Kevin when Catherine read that part, and his expression hadn't changed at all. He still looked totally vacant, with no recognition on his face or awareness of his surroundings.

JOCELYN: Do you know who else is here?

KEVIN: I don't care. I only know and feel you're with me. Funny how things change, excuse me for being impolite to your company.

CHAPTER 35

THE BEND IN THE ROAD

JOCELYN: So Kev, what's going on?

KEVIN: It's you and me, kiddo, and we are in the last bend now.

JOCELYN: What's that mean? Like a bend in the road?

KEVIN: It means you and I are coming to that place where I go ahead and wait for you, and I scout it out and you bitch about it. Sorry for using language in front of your company.

JOCELYN: It's Vicky and Catherine. They've heard it before.

KEVIN: But being a gentleman always matters, and I'm sorry. It's this time to be with you, so excuse my indelicacies.

JOCELYN: So, doll, do you know how long you have, or what's … Either tell me what you know, tell me what you want, or tell me what you think.

KEVIN: I think I'm trapped and sick of this, and I think you are hovering way too much. I love you, so I won't risk your wrath, but it's nevertheless true. This just goes on and on and on.

JOCELYN: So you know you're not dreaming. Do you also know that you're still in the hospital?

KEVIN: I'm at a wait station. Hospitals are for sick people. I'm not sick. I'm on my way home, just around the bend.

JOCELYN: You don't mean home in Santa Barbara, do you?

I knew what home he was talking about. I just didn't want to hear him say it.

KEVIN: I mean where I've always been headed. Home to be with God. I'm not meaning to be inflammatory. I know you're plenty mad at him. But in time I'm hoping this will be a gentle place for you and not the middle finger.

Catherine was laughing while writing "middle finger." He was right, I was plenty mad at God. Even now, when I hear stories of people who had a terminal illness, have a near-death experience, then come back and their illness is cured, I get mad at God all over again. Why didn't he do that for Kevin?

JOCELYN: He's right. I am mad at God. He knows that. You're correct. He could fix this and he's not.

KEVIN: But that doesn't mean I'm broken. How dare you see it as a failing on God's part. If I could have done anything, it would have been to do a better job of helping to let you see what I see, know what I know. It's all real. I have no doubts.

Kevin would try at times to talk to me about what he knew to be true and real about his deep faith in God and Jesus, but I wasn't ever really interested. It was his thing, not mine.

Kevin's concern for Jocelyn's anger with God struck me as an odd focus, given the circumstances.

JOCELYN: Do you know how much longer you have?

KEVIN: No, I don't know when I get my ripcord pulled to fly into a great welcoming. I hear you still trying to say, "It's not cruising level enough." We aren't at the drop site yet, but I'm ready, and you know me. You're not ready, so you are keeping me in the plane. I'm like "I'm leaping" and you're like "no, sir-ee."

He meant that he wouldn't die if I wasn't ready. Like always, how I felt was more important to him than how he felt. I panicked when he said that he was ready. I didn't want him to be ready to die. It wasn't that time yet.

JOCELYN: I don't really have any ability to stop you from jumping out of the plane. It's clearly not my choice.

KEVIN: No, but it's hard when we are so much together as one mind. So I can't communicate traditionally, but you and I are so of one mind, and yours is screaming "No!" You fight—you fight to the last breath, and I've never been a match for you. Uncle, Uncle, Uncle!

I know it's all love. I know, but I can't go if you are screaming "No!" I can't leave you if you aren't ready. I'm sorry, but it's been us together, thick, thin, and ripening in the middle. Good, bad, indifferent, we have slain so many dragons together, and you have always been the fire breather. I've always just followed, broom in hand, picking up the pieces. Don't make this your fight for me, for you, for the kids. There isn't a dragon here. You shoot me in such a deep way with your fierceness. You just tantrum. I thought the up-close version could get ugly, but the inside-to-inside one? I'm not messing with that!

Catherine is commenting here that "he is so hilarious" and is chuckling as she is writing. She feels his energy, and uses inflections as she relays it, so the printed word doesn't really capture the fullness of the conversation.

Jocelyn: I'm not sure what you mean by that, sweetie.

I realized what he meant right after I said this. When there was something that we needed to fight for in our lives, or something I felt strongly needed to go one way or another, I was fierce and relentless in doing whatever needed to be done to make it happen. He actually used to use the word "fierce" to describe me when I got like that, joking that he never wanted to be on the receiving end of it himself. That was what he was saying now—that while my fight for his life could look ugly from the outside—and there were several times over the last seven weeks when it had gotten ugly—it was nothing compared to him feeling it inside-to-inside.

KEVIN: As the other stuff has left me, my inside ears and heart listening have gotten much more acute. I hear what your heart says, not even your brain inside you. I hear pure Joc. I hear pure you. It really is heart-to-heart now. It's a blessing and a curse.

Catherine was chuckling at the "blessing and a curse" part. She wasn't laughing at me. Rather, it was like she was laughing with Kevin and his funny comment. I was really struck by her easy manner. This all seemed so natural, like we were just having a regular conversation.

JOCELYN: He's always kinda thought that about me. I've been a mixed bag from the beginning.

CHAPTER 36

YOUR PLAN IS FOOLHARDY

KEVIN: This latest plan is foolhardy, completely foolhardy. I'm like a piece of furniture. Don't move me around like an old comfortable chair you can't bear to part with. It's not what I want or what we discussed.

JOCELYN: What would you like me to do?

KEVIN: You play naïve, but there is culpability, and we both know it. So stop pretending. Please, for all of us.

CATHERINE: What's "culpability"?

JOCELYN: You know, like when you are culpable. He's saying I'm partially responsible for this.

KEVIN: Not partially.

This made me feel awful. I had been trying to do what I thought he wanted by getting him to Santa Barbara sooner, but I couldn't make it happen. I was finally bringing him home, and he was saying I was responsible for his situation. I had hardly left his side and now I felt like he was chewing me out over it. I was sad and frustrated at the same time. I thought maybe he had just given up, and I wasn't ready for him to give up. I certainly hadn't, and I didn't want him to either.

JOCELYN: Are you intentionally trying not to get better? Because you aren't participating at all, and you were before. Have you just given up?

KEVIN: It's so like you to blame me. No, I haven't given up. I have continual diminished capacities. Get your head out of your own ass!

Ouch! That hurt.

JOCELYN: I can't believe you said that to me!

KEVIN: Sorry.

JOCELYN: No, it's all right. You can do whatever you want at this stage.

KEVIN: Not unkindly. But you keep thinking I'm not trying. Think how insulting that is. I'm not picking it off with you. I'm saying facts is facts, Missus. The truth is, I'm deteriorating more and more. I can't fight, try, or do whatever to find my way out of this.

The contentious tone of their exchange waned. Kevin really was struggling with getting Jocelyn to accept his imminent death, but she was having none of it.

JOCELYN: The reason I ask that, sweetie, is because when we got to rehab a couple of weeks ago, you were much more able to follow commands and participate. Now you're just—you can't do anything. I didn't know whether it was because you'd given up trying or … I didn't know why it was like that. I didn't know whether it was a physiological thing, or whether you have given up trying because you don't see the point.

KEVIN: I suffered loss. My brain is eroding. I can't make myself do something. I send it directions, but it's like shouting in an empty room. You're frustrated? Think about me.

JOCELYN: I don't want you to be frustrated, honey.

KEVIN: You would last twelve minutes in this condition. It's not me pulling back. God knows, I'm stuck in this body that I have about ten percent control over—if even ten.

JOCELYN: Do you know when I'm with you?

KEVIN: Absolutely! That's what I was saying earlier. I hear your heart. It's entwined in mine. I hear inside you, the things you won't even whisper to yourself. Not bad stuff, but the heart of you. I've always known you were this "mush-loving center candy" with some hard crusty coating at times.

JOCELYN: Mush-loving center candy?

KEVIN: Ha, ha, ha! But now I see so much more. It's like the rest of the crap has melted in between and I see your heart. I feel your heart just holding me in ways no one ever has, can, or will, and I'm so grateful to you. I'm so blessed. I am a rich man beyond compare. I have had such an incredible life, wife, family, and everything—everything.

Catherine, Vicky and I were all crying by now.

Although we were all moved and crying, Jocelyn looked at Vicky angrily and said, "Stop it, Vicky. Stop crying!" Jocelyn's defenses were eroding and she refused our compassion or empathy. It was apparent she didn't want the floodgates of her emotions to open and risk being swept into full despair.

KEVIN: And just because you don't want to be a baby, let this lady cry if she wants to. Stop directing traffic. It's just old. We are coming up to my "home stretch." Let me say it—let me shout it!

Let me do whatever this strange thing is. But my love knows no end, no end, no end. Do you hear me? My love has no end—no damn end. None! Okay, are we agreed? Because it always ends up here, same place. Me talking to you, and you trying to override it. "Same old, same old" in the most loving way. Please, I'm not saying it with anything other than deep love and every fiber that remains of my being. "Jocelyn, I love you." So this isn't the Kevin Show, so let it be. Let that love just speak. It is, and you are the one who taught me it. What am I waiting for? To just let you know my love is enough to let me go. It's enough. It really is so much bigger than this. Please, you know in your soul I would never choose to leave you. Okay, who needs tissues now, ladies? Tissues?

Kevin was trying to add some humor here. We were all sobbing now, and he knew it.

JOCELYN: You know I love you. You know I love you best of all.

KEVIN: I know you do. I've never for one second—well, maybe a few—doubted that. Do you know what an incredible ride we've had? Top down, wind in our hair, me in my glasses. So this outdoors, strapped to a chair, isn't it—not for me, not for you, and most of all, not for the kids. Propping dad in the corner isn't sufficient. It just isn't.

He was teasing me with that "maybe a few" comment. Kevin always wore sunglasses when he drove, and I used to comment on how cool he looked driving with them on. I have many pictures taken from the passenger seat of him wearing his sunglasses as he drove. Every time we took a trip, I'd snap a picture of him in his sunglasses. He would sigh and say, "Oh, Joc."

JOCELYN: So if I said it was okay if you left, you'd go? Do you have any control over that?

I was hoping he wasn't going to say yes. I was afraid that, given the conversation so far, if I said it was okay for him to leave, he would literally die right there on the patio.

KEVIN: You know, I know you well enough to believe it isn't what you say that I need to understand.

JOCELYN: You know what's funny? I was just thinking I would say that, but wouldn't really mean it.

KEVIN: That's the heart part. I told you, I'm not listening to words. Heck, I have an inside track to you even you don't have. But that's what I'm waiting for, to know that you know you'll be okay. You aren't there yet. It's not a judgment, it's a reality.

He was right. I wasn't okay with the end coming so much sooner than we had anticipated.

JOCELYN: I don't think I'd ever be okay with it, but that shouldn't stop you. I can't make myself want that.

KEVIN: It isn't like there is some clock I can just punch out either. So we are both like in some awful B-rated movie, and I'm no hero and you're no heroine. So we are doing this whole noble routine, but it's still B-rated. So I say, "Don't go for popcorn or switch theaters." I say let that love be our 24-hour all-real scene, because it is. This is just some bad, bad life-imitating hell. So we are both in the crapper together.

JOCELYN: I really mean it when I say I want you to go when you're ready, and not when you think I'm ready. I really mean that. I don't want you to wait for me to be ready. That's not fair, and I wouldn't do that to you. I mean that. I'm not just saying it.

I did really mean it, even though it was the last thing in the world I wanted. I was both heartbroken and terrified at that same time.

KEVIN: I know you mean it. Now we are at hour 15 and it's becoming a little clearer to both of us. This is a non-salvageable situation.

JOCELYN: I know it is. I know you are never going to get better. Do you know that I know that?

KEVIN: I know you do.

JOCELYN: Do you understand all the conversations I've had with the doctors and nurses? I mean, you know I realize you aren't going to recover, right?

> *I knew Kevin was never going to fully recover. It wasn't "if" he was going to die, but "when." I wasn't ready, and I never would be, but I didn't want him trying to stay alive just because I wasn't ready for him to die.*

CHAPTER 37

I'm Speaking From My Heart

KEVIN: I know you understand that I'm not going to recover, but you keep holding on to not wanting to let yourself believe it. In your shoes, I wouldn't be able to know it that way inside either. That's how love is. So I'm not saying I'm staying because you have me handcuffed. I don't even get it myself that I'm like this and still breathing. It's ridiculous. It's past the point of ridiculous. So I'm not laying blame or anything. I'm as perplexed with what little brain cells I have how this is even physically possible. I'm speaking not from my grey matter but my heart, and it's strong and beating.

Up until this point, besides crying and laughing at what Kevin was saying, Catherine had just been reading the writing. When he talked about speaking from his heart, her eyes flew open and she had an "oh, wow!" look on her face.

JOCELYN TO
CATHERINE: Clearly, from your face there's some significance which I'm missing.

CATHERINE: I think what he's saying is that the part of him that's talking isn't in his brain. That's what I'm finding significant. I'm hearing this for the first time, just like you. He's not communicating with me from his brain. It's his heart that's talking. That his vocabulary isn't even in his head. Whether he has his mind fully functioning or not, he's saying that he's speaking from his heart. It's almost as miraculous of a statement for me to hear as him saying, "Tap my fingers," then waking himself up. I mean, maybe he is saying something that none of us have ever thought of. That it truly is our heart or soul that lives on, and that it has nothing to do with our brain.

JOCELYN: Kevin, are you speaking from your heart, not your mind?

KEVIN: Yes!

JOCELYN: Does Catherine have it right in what she said?

KEVIN: Yes!

CATHERINE: I mean, do you know what that means for all of us?

JOCELYN: No.

Catherine, Vicky and I were all crying again.

CATHERINE: I mean, I don't know what it means either, but do you know what I'm referring to?

JOCELYN: No. I'm clueless about crap like that.

CATHERINE: I'm just saying that as a concept, it just means … My mind doesn't even know what to do with it. All of my understanding of reality has just been tilted on end. Do you know what I'm saying?

JOCELYN: No, I never understood anything like that.

I knew that Catherine was into spiritual stuff and was familiar with concepts I had never heard of and didn't care about. I'm clueless when it comes to spiritual concepts. People who are into the "spiritual thing" speak a completely different language, and I don't speak spiritual. Catherine seemed so moved and in awe, but I was just confused.

CATHERINE: He's saying that he's talking from his heart. Usually when people talk from the heart, it's still coming through their head. The brain is the apparatus. He's saying, "No, no, no, this is not the apparatus." I don't even know what that means.

JOCELYN: So it's coming from your heart and not your head?

KEVIN: I don't have a head to come from, and I'm clearer than I've ever been. So this toilet of a situation has been a gift. A gift to know you from the inside out. It's a gift to hold you from the inside out. It's a blessing from God. I don't need confirmation, because my heart is one with yours. There is not one speck of doo-doo between us. And girlfriend, when you get here, I'm wearing you out!

Despite the seriousness of what he was saying, that this horrible situation had been a gift, I laughed when he said, "I'm wearing you out!"

Now I clearly grasped the head versus the heart concept. He was literally communicating from his heart rather than his mind. He was resolved and at peace. Unbelievably, he was grateful because he was now able to experience his connection with and love for Jocelyn even more. I thought this must be what happens when all our barriers, self-protection, and ego disappear. It must truly be unconditional love he was talking about.

CHAPTER 38

WHAT DO YOU WANT TO DO?

JOCELYN: So, doll, what do you want to do from this point? You know we are going home tomorrow. I'm going to get some help to take care of you. I've said for weeks that I would take the best care of you for as long as you have. From my heart, that's how I really feel, and I think I'm doing a pretty good job. That's what I need to do to feel like I'm okay with this—take care of you.

KEVIN: I don't want the kids to see me like this. It's okay part-time but not in our house. It's just not okay, and you can't pretty it up. I'm sorry. I know it's the sacred cow on the table of the non-meat eaters. But look how hard it was with my dad. This is a million times worse.

JOCELYN TO
CATHERINE: His dad stayed with us a few months and it was grueling.

> *When Kevin's dad stayed with us after he fell and hit his head, it was really hard to take care of him in our home and still have it be normal for the kids. His dementia meant he was disoriented and agitated all the time.*

KEVIN: Make the call. You know there are options, and your strong-headedness isn't enough to inflict this on our children. It was so apparent with dad. So now what about this, scale to scale? Come on.

> *I knew what call he was talking about. Santa Barbara has a hospice care facility called Serenity House. The Visiting Nurses Association I set up the home health care with also runs Serenity House. They had talked to me about the Serenity House option when I was making the plan to bring Kevin home, but I didn't even want to consider taking him there because the only way you leave Serenity House is in a body bag. I always knew Kevin didn't want to die at home. We had talked about it before the surgery, and he had told me that when it came to the end, he wanted me to take him to Serenity House.*

JOCELYN: I didn't love your dad like I love you. It's different.

KEVIN: Put it on a scale. It's not even about love. It's about stress and reality. Dad? Me? What do you think it's going to be like for them? I deserve dignity, and that's not dignity seeing myself in—well, I'll spare all of us the details.

JOCELYN: I know you don't like it when I wipe your tooshie, but I don't mind. It's just a butt.

KEVIN: Bend over and have someone wipe you and say that!

> *I laughed here. Since Kevin couldn't do anything for himself, I had insisted on performing all his personal hygiene instead of the nurses doing it. I wanted to take care of him. Kevin was always really private about stuff like that. I had thought that if he was aware of what I was doing, he would be mortified. Since we had kids, wiping butts wasn't a new concept for me.*

JOCELYN: I miss your sense of humor. I miss you.

KEVIN: You're not equipped to be this helpless. I miss you, but here is what I'm saying now that the rest is leaving. Jocelyn, I have you so much closer in so many ways. I see your heart from the inside, and I'm not talking undivided attention. I'm saying that my heart, or soul—I'm not sure which—is how I sense everything now, because the penthouse is closed for business.

Catherine looked perplexed at his "penthouse" comment.

JOCELYN TO
CATHERINE: He means his brain. That's what he means.

CHAPTER 39

THIS IS NONNEGOTIABLE

JOCELYN: I already have it all set up to bring you home tomorrow. How about you come home for a bit, then I'll move you to Serenity House? How does that sound? Is that okay with you?

KEVIN: Can you see if plans can be changed? If you take me home, then I know you—it's gonna take a crowbar to get you to get me out. So make some calls. Try. Try for us, for our kids. You can still be my sleepover buddy.

Catherine looked at me confused when he made the sleepover buddy comment.

JOCELYN: I sleep here.

CATHERINE: Oh, you do?

JOCELYN: That's why my back is killing me.

Because I had been sleeping with Kevin in his hospital bed for the last seven weeks, my body hurt so much that I limped around like an old woman. I slept with him for two reasons. First, if he had any moments of clarity, I wanted to be there for them. Second, we had been sleeping together for almost 27 years, and I wanted to keep sleeping together until the day he died.

JOCELYN: Do you have anything you want to say to the kids?

KEVIN: There isn't anything besides how proud I have been to be their dad and how sorry I am to have it end this way. But I'm going to be watching and loving them for every second of every moment. Tell them they have been a gift and there isn't one second I'd have traded. I don't have a single regret. Tell them I'm so proud and so bursting full of love, I'm going into high-octane angel mode when I get my wings.

JOCELYN: How about I take you home and I commit to two weeks or less?

KEVIN: How about this is nonnegotiable? It's ridiculous.

JOCELYN: Kevin, everything is negotiable. I've already lined it all up, and I think the kids ...

KEVIN: You can move hell and high water, so don't give me that dance. We've tangoed too many times for that to work.

> *He was right. I'm a "fixer" by nature. I knew I could make it happen if I wanted to, but I didn't want to. I wanted to stick with the plan I'd already made. I wanted him to come home. As we were driving out of our driveway to the hospital seven weeks ago, I had an irrational fear that it would be the last time Kevin ever drove out of our driveway. At the time, I just thought it was my anxiety and nervousness over the surgery. I didn't want Kevin to never come back to our home. It just felt so wrong.*

JOCELYN: I'm not sure I can fix it at this late hour, but I'll try. But if I can't ...

> I thought, "Oh, good Lord, here we go with the lawyers." The last writing involved a lot of negotiation. How would he ever get her to accept that he was really dying?

CHAPTER 40

MAKE THE CALL

KEVIN: A phone call, and I want priority on the first bed. No two weeks, no two days. No. Limit the collateral damage on our kids.

JOCELYN: If I call and they don't have space, I don't have another choice.

KEVIN: Okay, but you haven't called, have you?

JOCELYN: If I call and they don't have space, I'm going to have to take you home until they do.

I really had no intention of changing the plan. I didn't even want to try.

KEVIN: Okay, but I want you to know I'm all "heart ears," so get your phone out in my presence. Let's make the call.

JOCELYN: You know I would do anything for you.

KEVIN: Then dial.

Catherine was snickering here, because I was clearly stalling and Kevin was calling me out on it. I so didn't want to make that call.

JOCELYN: I would. Anything. You know that.

KEVIN: Then dial. Please, just dial. Please, come on. You are always the engine. Get your phone out. Don't turn stupid on me. I'm not buying it, lady.

JOCELYN: The kids are going to wonder why I'm doing this.

I was trying to think of ways to talk him out of it.

KEVIN: Tell them the doctors say the amount of care and stress has got to be considered, and your dad was very clear all along that he didn't want to have your home turned into a center for the dying. This is not new information, and it's not information you are hearing for the first time, so don't pretend it is. It was something we hoped would be avoidable, but here we are. Don't be afraid. You aren't afraid, and don't act like you'd ever let the kids' reaction dictate to you what you know is best for our family. I'm asking for a phone call.

JOCELYN: I'll do it. I give you my word. I'll do it, I promise. As soon as … I'll do it.

KEVIN: Sooner. I know your tactics. Get your phone out.

I wanted to wait until the writing was over, then mull it over before I did it. I knew the longer I waited, the less likely it would happen before 10:00 in the morning. It was already mid-afternoon. I was stalling.

JOCELYN: Do you want me to do it right this second?

KEVIN: Yes, yes!

JOCELYN: I don't have a phone.

Vicky said I could use her phone, pulled it out, and handed it to me. Traitor!

Kevin was as firm as Jocelyn was resistant. It was like being in the middle of an argument. Even though their bickering didn't involve me personally, it was uncomfortable to relay his responses. Clearly Jocelyn was angry at being told what to do, much less being challenged. She would definitely not be overridden.

JOCELYN: You really do know me, don't you?

KEVIN: And if it's meant to be, it will be. Okay?

JOCELYN: I'm doing it right this second.

KEVIN: Great.

I was slightly pissed off that he was pressing me to do it right then. I called 411 to get the number.

JOCELYN: You can listen. Do you want to listen?

I was a bit peeved that he didn't trust me to do it, but he was right. I wouldn't have made the call if he wasn't forcing my hand by listening.

KEVIN: Yes. It's my prerogative.

411: City and state, please.

JOCELYN: Santa Barbara, California.

411: What listing, please?

JOCELYN: Serenity House. Santa Barbara Serenity House.

KEVIN: You are my champion!

411: Thank you. I'm checking in Santa Barbara, California, under "Serenity House," and nothing with that name is coming up.

JOCELYN: How about Visiting Nurses Association?

411: Okay, thank you. Your call is being connected.

Ringing...

JOCELYN: I didn't want to do this, you know.

KEVIN: I know.

JOCELYN: I'm only doing it because you are making me.

I was crying again now. This was the last call I ever wanted to make.

KEVIN: I don't want to either, but trust me. It will only be a minute.

HOSPICE: Good afternoon, Visiting Nurses and Hospice Care. How may I direct your call?

JOCELYN: Hi. Can I talk to Admissions, please?

HOSPICE: In home health or hospice?

JOCELYN: Hospice.

At this moment, I felt completely defeated. The fight was over. This phone call signified that the end was near, and we all knew it.

HOSPICE: I'll transfer you.

JOCELYN: Thank you.

Hospice answered.

JOCELYN: Hi, my name is Jocelyn McIvers and I'm with my husband ...

HOSPICE: Yes.

They knew who I was because I had lined up the Visiting Nurses to come to our home and had arranged the hospital bed and all the supplies I would need to take care of Kevin through them.

JOCELYN: I've been told that it would be better if we considered the Serenity House option. I'm wondering whether it's too late to make that change, if you have space there, and what I would need to do to facilitate that.

KEVIN: Go, champ!

HOSPICE: I would actually have to initiate that. I will follow up and check with them to see if they have a bed available. Would this still be for tomorrow?

JOCELYN: If you could make that work, yes. It's just kind of become clear, just more today, that I don't think the home is going to be a viable option, unfortunately.

I'm crying as I'm talking to this poor woman. I'm guessing she has heard a lot of crying spouses over the years.

HOSPICE: Okay, Jocelyn. Even if you were to think of Serenity House as the place to help look after him, or for the possible transition to see if there's a chance to bring him home, you could consider it that way too.

JOCELYN: I don't think that is going to happen, but thank you for the cheery thought.

Hospice talked about how much it would cost and other details.

JOCELYN: That's all fine. Money isn't an issue.

Kevin made a great living as a mediator, but when he was re-diagnosed a few months back, we got a cash advance on part of his life insurance policy in order to do all the things that were on his bucket list for his last year of life without having to worry about the cost. Since that wasn't happening, I was using the insurance money to pay for the private nurses he had in the hospital and the W Hotel in Westwood where we stayed for seven weeks. (I could have bought a car with that hotel bill.) Now the money would cover hospice. I was grateful that money wasn't an issue at this point, but so sad that we were using it on Kevin dying, instead of doing all those things he always wanted to do but now wouldn't get to do. It was all so unfair.

HOSPICE: I have your contact number, Jocelyn. So if I may, I will reach out to Serenity House, see what's available, and call you right back.

I was so hoping they wouldn't have a bed, so I could bring Kevin home.

CHAPTER 41

I DIDN'T WANT TO DO THAT

KEVIN: See? That wasn't too hard. Thank you, my sweet love. I'm so grateful. Breathe, breathe, breathe.

I was practically hyperventilating at this point.

JOCELYN: Are you satisfied? [*I sounded pissed off.*] I didn't want to do that. [*I was crying.*] I must really love you, because I just did something I didn't want to do, and I never do something I don't want to do.

KEVIN: I'm just so thankful to be heard.

JOCELYN: Now you made me feel guilty. Of course I heard you! Just because I don't want to listen doesn't mean I don't hear you. I say that with love in my heart. I didn't want to do that. I'll do it for you, because I really love you. I'll do what you want. And if you really love me, don't just hang on because you think I can't take it, because if I can take seven weeks of this, I think I can take anything.

KEVIN: No, I know. And I know, heart-to-heart, you didn't want to. That's why I'm saying thank you. I've never doubted your love. I just never have, ever. Don't doubt mine!

JOCELYN: Of course I don't doubt it. I don't like being forced to do things I don't want to do though. You know I like to be in control of everything.

KEVIN: How do you think I feel, tied into a chair?

JOCELYN: With a diaper.

KEVIN: Okay, enough with the details.

JOCELYN: I made the call, all right? They are going to see whether they have a bed. It's $15,000 a month, and we can do that, all right?

KEVIN: You are the bravest woman I know. And I'll try to keep the costs down.

We all laughed, but it wasn't really funny. He was trying to make me laugh because he knew I was sad.

JOCELYN: Don't worry about the money.

KEVIN: I'm kidding, I'm kidding, I'm kidding!

JOCELYN: That's not funny.

KEVIN: Hey, can't get out alive anyway. Laugh … I love the sound of your laugh.

JOCELYN: I love the sound of yours too.

KEVIN: Yes, we had 'em.

JOCELYN: Yeah, we did. I don't think we are going to have many more though, honey.

KEVIN: Never underestimate my abilities post-mortem.

Despite Kevin's attempts to encourage and humor Jocelyn, this was painful for me to watch. The fight was over. Her love finally allowed her to do for him what some short hours before she had been walled off from doing. All her love, care, and need to bring him home weren't going to work.

JOCELYN: Can I talk to you when you are gone? You always told me you didn't want to do that, but can I do that? Not that that would have stopped me, of course.

> *Before Kevin went in for surgery, I asked him whether he would try to talk to me when he was gone. My sister believed that Catherine could communicate with dead people. I didn't really believe it at the time. But since I was talking to my practically brain-dead husband, and had already talked to him through Catherine when he was in a coma, I was pretty certain we could talk after he died if he wanted to. It made all this more palatable, to think that our relationship would go on even after he died.*

KEVIN: I can still be heart-to-heart! I didn't believe this was possible. In a way, I like it almost as well.

JOCELYN: You know you're my treasure. I'm sorry you're going through all this.

KEVIN: So okay, no freaky ghost crap. I understand this is the most natural thing. Could have tricked me, I never heard about this in any of those seminars or books.

> *Kevin had told me some pretty amazing things that he had studied in those religious texts he was always reading and from seminars he attended, like people raising babies from the dead in Africa. I thought that what was happening here with him and Catherine wasn't nearly as much of a stretch as raising a baby from the dead.*

KEVIN: It's like, I knew you were my most beautiful blessing. But it's almost like I knew you at 37%, and now I'm at 87%.

JOCELYN: Why only 87%?

KEVIN: Because I know you like to keep me guessing. And look, you dialed that phone, the hardest call of your life. I get it. I get it. So I think I'm saying I knew you had it in you even when you didn't. It's a heart-to-heart thing. Death isn't going to break that. No way! Nope. Okay? 91%. If I could save the cost of transport, I would.

The percentages were unclear to me. I didn't know whether they related to his brain functionality or the level of their heart-to-heart connection. They obviously loved each other without constraint, and this love and Kevin's faith kept them afloat in this awful limbo. As we sat there waiting for hospice to call back, he kept the conversation going to distract her.

CHAPTER 42

IT'S WHOLLY SPIRIT

KEVIN: What a glorious day. A breeze, you and me. Okay, awkward chaperones, but God's grace is all around. Not that old-time Jesus stuff that inflames you, but the holy in Holy Spirit. Brilliant insight! It's not "Holy," it's "Wholly Spirit," and that's what we are connecting through.

> *He was right. That old-time Jesus fundamentalist Christian stuff inflamed me. It just seemed so pompous and pretentious to me. I knew a lot of supposed Christians who weren't Christlike. When Kevin first became sick, I used to wonder out loud why it was happening to him when he was such a wonderful man and not some worthless loser pond scum of the earth. One of our Christian friends actually told me that if I had loved God more than Kevin and not vice versa, maybe this wouldn't be happening. So yeah, I was soured on that "old-time Jesus stuff," as he put it.*

JOCELYN: How do you know it's "Wholly," and not "Holy"?

CATHERINE: Because he spelled out W-h-o-l-l-y.

JOCELYN: Huh! Maybe "Holy Spirit" is really "Wholly Spirit." Maybe they got it wrong all those years? Really!

KEVIN: Down, down, down. You could run with this! But I really mean it. Wholly as in all of me. Wow! Mr. Potato Head gets a new part.

JOCELYN: So now that you've had a bit of your own epiphany, you don't have to hang around for me. I really mean it, okay?

KEVIN: Not trying to or not to.

JOCELYN: Good, because I felt guilty before. You made it sound like I was a tie that was binding you to a place you didn't want to be. I'm glad I'm not.

> *I was feeling so guilty already for agreeing to all those surgeries and procedures of the last seven weeks. I felt guilty before this writing, but now I felt even worse. I felt like I had wronged the man I loved, not only by all those medical decisions but also in not wanting to let him die in the way he wished and trying to take him home even though he didn't want to go. I wanted him to feel he could die whenever the time was right and not be concerned about me being ready or not, because I knew I would never be ready.*

KEVIN: No! I wasn't shackled. I'm convicted, but not shackled. If we were in charge, we'd be on a fabulous trip. Sex on the beach!

JOCELYN: All right!

KEVIN: Had to give you a little thumb's up. Next ecstasy? Well, we both will see. You are a finer woman by the second. Oh, here we sit …

> *I used to take him outside on the patio to this same spot every day to get fresh air and sit in the sun. Even though we were in the center of Westwood, it was really a peaceful place. It was so nice to escape the medicinal-smelling hospital and just be alone together. I'd sit in his lap with my head on his*

shoulder and pretend he was healthy and we were just sitting on a bench in a park, enjoying a beautiful day together.

Jocelyn had climbed back on Kevin's lap facing him and had her arms and legs wrapped around him. In that moment it looked like the most natural thing in the world. He revealed no awareness she was even there, but heart-to-heart he said they were closer than close. Their relationship had weathered unspeakable challenges. When she placed her heart against his, they were literally heart-to-heart. I said a silent prayer for God to grant them more time to love each other.

JOCELYN: I'm going to miss you. But I miss you already, so it's kind of been good practice.

KEVIN: It's not a dress rehearsal. You are my love. Our love story isn't over when I get that homecoming call, and it isn't over for you either. One thing we know is our love is bigger than anything that gets thrown at us. My inner eyes see you with such clarity. There is nothing more beautiful. Top that, God, I double dare you—only kidding. A little comic relief while arrangements are being made. I know how to try to distract you, probably never successfully mastered it. Can't blame a guy for trying.

JOCELYN: You know Kevin, I always thought I got the better end of the deal and I still feel that way.

KEVIN: We both did.

JOCELYN: Only one of us gets the better end, and it's me. But thank you for the compliment.

KEVIN: Okay, last word as usual.

JOCELYN: No, I want you to have the last word.

KEVIN: Love. It's simple and it's everything. I can't speak with my mouth, and the tongue feels like it's twisted with a string pulling it, but the heart says love. The heart hears love. The heart is love. We are love. In the old-time religion, somebody ought to shout, "Can I get a witness?"

We all laughed.

KEVIN: Amen, sister.

JOCELYN: That was funny, Kevin.

KEVIN: When you got it, share it.

I know Kevin was trying to keep things lighthearted while we waited for hospice to call back.

Kevin had said it: "Love. It's simple and it's everything." So often taken for granted, love is for some people just another thing on a long list of "I should." We love because it's a rare gift, born out of the divine spirit of connection, soul, and what we are designed for. Kevin was about to lose his life, and he was crystal clear what was most important—love.

Throughout many thousands of pages in the writings, God speaks about love. "Love bears all," and Kevin and Jocelyn's situation was a living demonstration of that. We humans make love far more complicated with our ego, intellect, and fear. It was Jocelyn's love that let her make the call and accept what she never wanted to. Kevin was dying, but his love was soaring, deepening and enveloping her from the inside out.

CHAPTER 43

MORE ALIVE AND AWARE

JOCELYN TO
CATHERINE: Is there anything you want to ask him?

CATHERINE: I'm just still curious about the heart-speaking thing. Can you say anything about that?

KEVIN: Now that I have no brain relationships I'm in control of, I feel more alive and aware than ever. I haven't imagined it. I'm saying "heart"—maybe it's soul or spirit, I'm not sure. All I can say is from this experience, I know I'm not thinking or formulating this conversation in a way I ever have before. It's coming from a different place within me that's stronger and more alive and knowing than ever. You think a guy on such a short leash would feel threatened and fearful, but I just feel myself getting larger—sensation-wise, not body-wise.

JOCELYN: This is going to sound like a really rhetorical question, but I'm guessing at this point you don't want me to do chemotherapy. Is that a given?

The doctor and I had discussed doing the next round of chemo when Kevin got home. I was still hoping that he would recover enough to interact meaningfully with us again and all he needed was rest. The last scan hadn't shown any new cancer growth, so I wanted to start the chemo to give him the chance to live longer. I knew by this point in the writing that he would say no, and hospice wouldn't start it anyway. It was a stupid question to ask him. I guess I was still hopeful.

KEVIN: Will it kill me quicker? Nope, don't bother. I'm about cruising altitude. It's okay, you don't have to flinch, it's a reality. [*I was sitting on his lap, holding his hand, so he must have felt me flinching.*] We have been in reality's trenches and death grip, and this is the worst of it. When we stand hand in hand and face it, in your heart you are for the first time facing it, and my hand is in yours. My hand is in yours, but that limp thing is no match for my heart, which is in yours—and nothing is changing that. I thank you for being braver than brave. You never needed this test. Neither of us did.

We could and would have rather blissfully and ignorantly lived to be old and gray, and so I grayed before you. We didn't know what awaited us, and that's probably better, because I have no look backs, no would-have, should-have done it better. We did it. Everywhere. [*I snickered and commented here that this was an inside joke.*] And it's true, no breath held back. Thank you, my life, my love.

The heart doesn't have all that the feelings are, because how I love you is like multiplied to infinity and beyond. Who could have thought that, in the last days of my life, I'd just really, really be able to be blessed with loving you more. No limit here. I wish I could just sprout some wings here and now.

JOCELYN: Since you're tied to a chair that would be difficult. I think you are getting pneumonia again. They keep checking, but you aren't breathing as well as you should be.

He was coughing while we were doing the writing. I hated hearing him cough and suffer from labored breathing. When we left UCLA the next day, the doctor said Kevin did in fact have pneumonia again.

KEVIN: Don't try to intercept the inevitable. Details are just the details.

JOCELYN: If you go to Serenity House, they will just try to keep you comfortable. They won't treat you for anything.

KEVIN: It's what I want. Treatment is for recovery. My comfort is also comfort for all of us. I'm not doing it because of comfort. I'm just seeing that this is the best for all of us, in ways this nightmare hasn't given us. This has been a rough ride, and so comfort—mine, yours, and the kids'—is long overdue.

JOCELYN: Have you felt in pain or uncomfortable?

I was crying here again, but I pretty much cried throughout the whole writing. I was always worried that Kevin was in pain or uncomfortable and couldn't communicate it. That would have made this nightmare even worse for both of us.

KEVIN: I don't know that I'm in pain. My brain doesn't sense that way. Sometimes I do feel reflexes, and I'm like, "What was that?" But suffering pain? Nope.

JOCELYN: That's the most important thing to me. I just don't want you to be in pain, that's all. That's why I wanted to take you home and take care of you, because I think I could take care of you better than these yahoos.

KEVIN: But it's not like propping a few pillows. Let it be.

JOCELYN: Okay, I will. You have my word.

KEVIN: I know you are agreeing under duress. The record can show that.

JOCELYN: It doesn't matter why I'm agreeing to it. If that's what you want, that's what I'll do. I'll do it for you because I love you, not because I want to.

KEVIN: And because this isn't a new conversation.

JOCELYN: I know.

KEVIN: We have had it several times and in several variations. So know in your heart you are following MY (capital letters, notice) wishes—and as tough as that is, I know you love me enough to even do the impossible, the unthinkable.

JOCELYN: Which is what? Make that phone call? Let you go? I'm denser than you, Kevin.

KEVIN: Oh, it was the phone call. We aren't at 92% yet. We got 8% left.

JOCELYN: I'll take the 90th percentile.

KEVIN: You never would settle. I may be neurologically impaired, but you are Ms. 120%.

This was a joke between us. When our kids were young and we took them to the doctor for checkups, they used to say that they were in the 90th percentile for growing or reaching milestones, or whatever. I was always so excited. Kevin teased me about it and often commented about things being in the 90th percentile.

CHAPTER 44

PUT MY RING ON

KEVIN: Can you put my ring on a chain?

I kiss him here.

JOCELYN: It's on a chain on my neck. Do you want it on a chain on your neck?

KEVIN: I want it on me. Can you put the ring on a chain? I want it on me so I can just put all of that love into it—and when it's done, put it back on you.

I took it off my neck and put it on his finger.

JOCELYN: I just put it on your finger. Do you feel it?

KEVIN: No. That's the way this works. Sometimes I do, and mostly I don't.

JOCELYN: That makes sense in terms of your rehab. When you were basically in a coma, you kept pointing to my ring finger, then pointing to your ring finger, because you wanted your ring back on your finger. I put it on, but you got so skinny I had to take it off. But it's back on. Do you feel it now?

KEVIN: Yes.

JOCELYN: Right there?

> *I was touching his ring on his finger and moving it around so he could feel it.*

KEVIN: But you're right, I want it on a chain so it doesn't get lost.

JOCELYN: Your ring is on your finger and you've gained some weight back, so it's not going to be that easy to get it off. It won't get lost on your finger. Do you still want it on a chain, or can I leave it on your finger?

KEVIN: You can have them tape it for transport. It's important you have it. I just don't want it lost.

JOCELYN: Do you want me to put it back on your finger when you get to Santa Barbara?

KEVIN: Up to you. Finger or chain, I just want it to be on me until that final passing. I took an oath. I vowed to you, and I want it to the last breath. It's real, and the punch line is that even then we aren't parted. I know that.

> *Kevin only took his wedding ring off two times in our whole marriage. The first time was when he had his first surgery, right after he was initially diagnosed following our Hawaii trip in 2009. They had to cut it off his finger before the surgery because he couldn't get it off on his own. I had the ring repaired, and he put it back on and didn't take it off until the second surgery in 2013. I knew it meant a lot to him, but I didn't realize how much until, when he was basically unconscious, he would rub the wedding ring on my finger, then rub his empty ring finger.*

> It wasn't unusual for Kevin to bring up their wedding vows. He indicated that there would be "no death do them part." What I found interesting was his concern about his wedding ring. For

centuries we have passed down the family jewelry and heirlooms. I wondered whether he was directing our attention to this being more than a tradition, perhaps sowing a deeper purpose which we failed to notice or understand. Maybe jewelry, objects, or other special mementos hold love energy in them. For example, it wasn't just Grandma's wedding ring we received, but all the love that she and Grandpa shared. Maybe those things bequeathed to us are far more special than just symbols or treasures. Maybe those items are imbued with the energy of the heart.

KEVIN: Those busy phone calls are being made.

JOCELYN: How do you know that?

KEVIN: The amazing Kev.

JOCELYN: Do you feel your ring now, honey?

KEVIN: I feel you, which is better than a ring. I'm just impeccable to my word.

JOCELYN: What's that mean? Yeah, you are like that, aren't you?

KEVIN: I took my vow and promise to you 150%.

JOCELYN: Let me scoot you back. Okay, ready? 1, 2, 3. I know you hate this.

Kevin was sliding down in his wheelchair. I was grunting from the exertion it took to scoot him up. He was literally "dead weight." I hate that expression, but now I really understood what it means.

CATHERINE: Do you want to go in? It's up to you.

JOCELYN: No, no. I'm just afraid he's going to fall out of the chair.

KEVIN: I'm fine wherever, just a comfortable piece of furniture.

We all laughed.

CHAPTER 45

A REMARKABLE MAN

CATHERINE: Kevin, you're a remarkable man.

VICKY: Extraordinary.

CATHERINE: Yep.

JOCELYN: Love of my life.

CATHERINE: You're teaching us some new things.

JOCELYN: He's always trying to teach me things, but I never want to listen.

KEVIN: No, but you did find the 411 moment. I'm officially impressed.

Kevin was always trying to teach me little life lessons, which I steadfastly refused to learn. It got to be kind of a running joke between us. For example, he signed up for a subscription to the National Geographic because he wanted the children and me to expand our minds and not read crappy gossip magazines. We refused to read the National Geographic. So when I was reading something mind-numbing and got up to go to the bathroom, fold the laundry or whatever, I would come back and the gossip rag was gone and the National Geographic was there in its place.

KEVIN: Never thought we'd be talking and being in this situation in the City of Angels. A cosmic joke, don't you think?

JOCELYN: Do you have anything else you want to say, love? I got out of this what I was hoping to. I mean, I could talk to you all day. I just feel overwhelmed, I really do. I want you to come home and … What I really want is you to get better, and I know that's not going to happen. I don't like not being in control of everything. It's discombobulating.

KEVIN: I know it's your worst nightmare, and you can't wake up and make it go away. I'm sorry.

> *The entire time we were at UCLA, I kept thinking that this had to be a nightmare and I would wake up one day and it would all go away. I think anyone who has a horrible situation thrust upon them without warning shares those same thoughts.*

JOCELYN: Don't be sorry, you didn't do anything wrong. I don't want you to feel sorry about anything. I'm sorry you got the surgery in the first place.

KEVIN: I'm not.

JOCELYN: How could you say that? You wouldn't be sitting here if we hadn't.

KEVIN: You don't know that. You forget the underlying condition was well under way. I'd have died a thousand times had I hurt you, the kids, or someone else. I think I had greater impairment than even I was willing to recognize.

> *Jocelyn sighed heavily here. I think she was feeling guilty. He wasn't just offering her forgiveness, but going head-to-head against her trying to shoulder responsibility for the horrible situation they were in.*

JOCELYN: Like what?

KEVIN: Lapses. Glitches. I don't know—like I was offline.

JOCELYN: Mentally or physically?

KEVIN: Like in my mind, not déjà vu, but like I was losing track of time and space a bit. Tiny, hardly perceivable to me, but I think that it was already really at work. I don't know where that cascade would have taken me, so please don't rehash our decisions. I'm not. You didn't support a wrong one.

JOCELYN TO
CATHERINE: I could tell he was having memory problems before the surgery.

CATHERINE: Oh, really?

JOCELYN: Yeah, but he always had a crappy memory.

KEVIN: Watch it! These were different.

> *One of the funny things about us as a couple was that Kevin always had a terrible memory, whereas I had a really great one. He was kind of like the absentminded professor. I thought he was having some memory issues before the surgery. But I'm not sure whether it wasn't just me projecting because I knew the cancer was back. Once you know that something is growing in there that shouldn't be, you tend to over-scrutinize things that you wouldn't ordinarily notice.*

JOCELYN: Oh, like when you were driving and stuff?

KEVIN: Yes, that was a concern to me.

JOCELYN: Then why did you keep driving?

KEVIN: Pride? I don't know. Denial? But I'd never have been able to have withstood hurting you, the kids, or anyone. So surgery wasn't necessarily a wrong choice. It didn't end up as we thought, but you can't say the surgery created this. If not this, then something else.

JOCELYN TO
CATHERINE: The oncologist said the end of this disease is really bad.

> *Kevin's neuro-oncologist told us that the end stage of brain cancer was really ugly. So maybe having him walk into surgery and never really wake up was a blessing in disguise. Or maybe not. I've gone back and forth on that countless times.*

KEVIN: So maybe the surgery was the silver lining in a black cloud. I just never anticipated this. We never anticipated this.

JOCELYN: I know, which is why when you say we've had this conversation before, that isn't really accurate, because we didn't anticipate this.

KEVIN: No, but I was clear I didn't want the kids to have to see me like this.

JOCELYN: That's true.

KEVIN: So no sugar coating. That was never debatable or misstated.

CHAPTER 46

I HEAR YOUR HEART

JOCELYN: Do you know what's going on around you, like when I talk about you going home or going to hospice? Can you process all that information? Or is it only when we're talking through Catherine that you can?

KEVIN: No, I can, but not by hearing you say it. It's that heart thing. I feel it, like I'm piped into your heart. Your thoughts aren't always audible to me, though they frequently are. But not brain-wise, heart-wise. That's what I meant, that I hear things in your heart that you haven't yet heard yourself.

JOCELYN: Like what?

There was no way I could let that comment slide. I wanted to know what he heard in my heart that I hadn't heard myself. Plus I wanted him to keep talking. Kevin had showed up for the first writing and again now, but I didn't know whether we would ever get to talk again or whether this might be our last time.

KEVIN: My time is short, and your heart is just as chatty as you are. [*Catherine is laughing.*] So I think you might need to kill a few trees for that list.

Kevin's right. I talk too much!

JOCELYN: Okay, just give me the Top Five. I'm curious. You can't throw that out there and not explain.

KEVIN: Kev's Top Five:

You say, "No! This is not fair." But then your heart says, "You will see him again. You can do this."

You say, "But I'm not ready. You can't have him!" And your heart says, "He isn't being taken from you. He is your always and forever fella."

JOCELYN: That's for sure.

I used to always refer to him as "my fella" to other people.

KEVIN: You say, "I'm not okay with this." Your heart says, "Love bears all things, and love is enough."

You say, "Damn you, God!" and other expletives. Your heart says, "God and Kevin will hold you in arms wide enough. Love is a blessing. Receive it."

He was right. I was cursing God and doubting his existence on a regular basis.

KEVIN: But mostly you try to make deals and feel defeated. Then your love overdrive kicks in, and it's like those scooters on the island without helmets. I hold on and you hold on, and we are free together. Open roads ahead, my love, only open roads. Relive it when you're sad.

On our honeymoon in the Bahamas, we rode scooters around the island without helmets on. We did that only once in the nearly 27 years we were together. He was right to remind me to relive it. It's a great memory.

Kevin could hear her thoughts and her heart. He even told her what he heard from her brain and how her heart held the real truth. Maybe our head is wired for resistance and complexity, fear and victimhood, whereas our heart is unwavering in its ability to love and be resilient. Our heart knows that our loved ones can never be taken from us or diminished by circumstances. In this way the mind, intellect, or ego holds one set of beliefs, whereas the heart has its own abiding presence, faith, truth, and eternal connection.

JOCELYN: I will. I'm sad now.

KEVIN: Yes, and it's expected.

JOCELYN: I'll relive it when I'm crying in my martini.

KEVIN: I think you need to plan your next big party, post-Kevin. Spare little expense.

JOCELYN TO
CATHERINE: We used to have those big Super Bowl parties. That's what he's saying.

KEVIN: This is different. Just for you and your posse.

JOCELYN: You mean like Cabo with Sue?

After Kevin got sick the first time, I went a few times to Cabo San Lucas, Mexico, with one of my best friends. We spent long weekends there just to relax by the pool, eat, and drink fruity alcoholic beverages with umbrellas in them while reading trashy novels. Just getting away for a few days and leaving my worries in Santa Barbara helped keep me sane during that time.

KEVIN: Yeah, those who can laugh with you one minute and drool the next.

JOCELYN TO
CATHERINE: He always said he didn't want to end up drooling.

Remember the last writing we had when I said, "You're drooling," and he said, "Oh, crap!"

CATHERINE: Oh, really? I don't remember.

JOCELYN TO
CATHERINE: Before he got sick again he said, "I just don't want to be like one of those old men who are leaning over in their wheelchairs, drooling."

KEVIN: That's why I like the head back position. Thanks, girls.

> *He was being funny. He was drooling a little. Because he had nerve damage on one side of his face and couldn't close the right side of his mouth all the way, it drooped. When I moved him up in his wheelchair, I also reclined it so he could lean back and have his head better supported, and also so he wouldn't drool.*

JOCELYN: That was great, Kevie. I feel better. Not really, but sort of.

KEVIN: It feels like us again. I know, it feels like us.

> *I so missed our back and forth banter and his dry wit. While this was such a strange situation in so many respects, as the conversation went on, it really felt like us again. It hadn't felt like that in seven weeks, except during the first writing with Catherine on the phone. When Catherine relays Kevin's energy, while it's in her voice, the intonations, inflections, phrases and word choices are all Kevin's. It's remarkable.*

> I had no sense of the amount of time Kevin and Jocelyn had left to be together. But I was so grateful that I had followed the inclination or intuition not to wait to do the writing until they got back to Santa Barbara. Jocelyn felt better, and Kevin was grateful for this reconnection and even related, "It feels like us again."

CHAPTER 47

IT'S A GO FOR KEVIN

My sister's phone rang. I knew who it was. My heart sank as she answered it.

JOCELYN: Kevin, here's the phone call. Hello?

HOSPICE: Jocelyn, this is Visiting Nurse Hospice Care. It's a go for Kevin to be able to come to Serenity House. I will be calling UCLA to make sure that the address is changed for the ambulance.

JOCELYN: You know, I'm riding in the ambulance, and I will make sure that they get there.

HOSPICE: I'll call and make sure they have the address. I just got the go-ahead now.

JOCELYN: Thank you for doing that.

HOSPICE: We'll cancel the medical equipment that was coming to the home.

JOCELYN: All right, thank you so much.

KEVIN: Thank you, my sweet love. Thank you, thank you. See? We let fate have it, and so we are set.

JOCELYN: I'm not happy about that. It's all right. Anyway, it's done.

KEVIN: Helmet off, my love. Don't have to risk head injury now. See girls? It's my girl. She did the impossible, and God was there to catch us both. I love you. Go to that place in your heart right now. No middle person, just you and me. Feel me! Our hearts are one. Thank you.

CATHERINE: Oh my God! I can't believe he is saying this.

KEVIN: And you can straddle me all you want there.

We all laughed. When Kevin and I used to sit out on the patio like we were now, I straddled his lap, with my legs wrapped around him so that our chests were pressed together and I could have my head on his shoulder. We were sitting like that now.

JOCELYN: Okay, all right …

My tone was like "overshare!" A therapist came out, looking to get us for physical therapy. I told him we were skipping it. No point now.

CATHERINE: Look at him patting you.

Kevin would always pat me, even when he was unconscious. I put his arm around me and he rubbed his hand on my back and patted it.

JOCELYN: He always does that. That's why I always think there's hope. You know, he hugs me and stuff. Up until recently, whenever I said, "I love you," he would say "love you" back.

KEVIN: Love always finds a way. Hope is a past destination. Love is the address, and we are love. Thank you, my sweet, sweet love. Thank you. Thank you for doing the hardest thing I've ever asked. Lovingly—kicking and railing, but lovingly.

JOCELYN: I've changed my spots now, huh?

KEVIN: No, I wouldn't go that far, and I never would ask you. What did we do to merit such blessings? I don't know, but I say thank you, God, and your son too.

Don't forget about my ring! It doesn't end my promises. I'll be just around the bend, but waiting. So know that.

JOCELYN: I have your ring on your finger. I'm riding in the ambulance with you, so don't worry—it won't go anywhere.

KEVIN: I love you.

JOCELYN: I love you too, very much. More than the sun and the moon and the stars.

I would always tell him and our kids that I loved them more than the sun, the moon, and the stars.

KEVIN: And any galaxies yet to be discovered. Wonderful. If I could sigh, I would. My whole Wholly Spirit says thank you.

JOCELYN: He shouldn't have to thank me for doing what he wants. He shouldn't. I'm sorry I did that to you. I apologize. You shouldn't have to thank me for doing what you wanted.

KEVIN: Don't back door the gratitude. Take it.

JOCELYN: All right, love.

KEVIN: It's important for me to say these things. I know you know, but it's you constantly third-, fourth-, and fifth-guessing.

JOCELYN: It's true. You're right.

KEVIN: So this is no more guesses. Homeward bound, me and my lady. We are going to blow the doors off this place and never look back.

JOCELYN: You mean UCLA? Yep, me too. I'm never coming back here to Westwood as long as I live, and I never want to stay at another W Hotel.

While Westwood is nice for L.A., and the W is a great hotel, they would have bad juju for me for the rest of my life.

KEVIN: Never say never. But hopefully our shadows won't darken these doors again.

CHAPTER 48

DON'T LET THEM MESS
WITH MY EYES

JOCELYN: Can you see me with your eye, Kevin? Can you see me? Do you have any vision?

CATHERINE: I swear to you … Honestly, you are so … I mean, I was writing this before …

Catherine lifted her clipboard and showed me what was written already. It was:

KEVIN: Don't let them mess with my eyes, let them decide up there.

JOCELYN: Oh, wow!

CATHERINE: He was saying, "Don't let them mess with my eyes, let them decide up there." I was writing, "let them decide up there" when she asked him if he could see with his eye.

This was a perfect example of what he was saying about hearing me through my heart and knowing my thoughts. I was thinking about his eyes and whether he could see, and he

*answered my question before I asked it. It was freaky, but then
again this whole experience had been unbelievable, so I guess I
shouldn't have been surprised.*

JOCELYN TO
CATHERINE: You know why? Because this eye [*his right eye*] was
stitched shut and they're taking the stitches out today. I told
them that because of quality of life, I wanted him to be able to
see us if he could. So they are taking the stitches out.

KEVIN: I can see periodically, just flashes.

JOCELYN: I'd like to take the stitches out of your right eye, so that
eye can see. Is that okay with you?

KEVIN: Sure.

JOCELYN: Like you're going to say "no" now, after all the other
concessions I've made.

KEVIN: But not here.

JOCELYN: Yes, they are doing it here.

*I didn't think they could do it at hospice. It really bothered
me to think he would die with one eye stitched shut.*

KEVIN: Okay, get on it.

JOCELYN: Is there a reason you don't want it done here?

KEVIN: It's just invasive.

JOCELYN: It's not. It's 20 seconds.

KEVIN: Let them do it, if you insist.

JOCELYN: I do.

KEVIN: So many concessions. Gotta give you this one. Not sure
I can see, but it's worth a try.

JOCELYN: That's what I think. And if you can't see, I'll just tape it shut and we won't worry about it.

KEVIN: Okay. Mr. Potato Head. Fondly, I am your servant in all things and you are my heart in all things. I think it's enough for now. We can touch any time our hearts are one. I love you! Homeward bound. Me and my lady. Helmets off.

JOCELYN: Thanks a lot, honey.

I was giving him little kisses all over his face now. I always used to do that, and he would laugh and say I was slobbering all over him like a dog.

I knew things were coming to a close for the writing, and I wanted to keep the conversation going. I didn't know whether we would ever talk again, although I hoped we would. Unfortunately, it was over.

GOD: Go with God.

CHAPTER 49

ACCEPTING BUT NOT READY

Jocelyn

The writing had lasted several hours and Catherine had gone round trip from Santa Barbara to UCLA, which was at least another three hours. I tried to pay her for her time, but she refused. Honestly, I would have given her any amount she asked for, because what she had given me was priceless—the ability to connect again with my fella—to laugh, talk, and just be us.

More importantly, this writing changed the plans I had made to take Kevin home, and he was now going where he wanted for his last days. I was happy and devastated at the same time. Happy that we had connected, and devastated to hear, directly from Kevin, that the end was much nearer than I thought. I wasn't ready. I was accepting, but not ready.

After the writing, we wheeled Kevin back to his room. I had missed touching base with the doctor who was going to discuss the MRI results with me. I already knew what those results would show because Kevin had told me that the end was near. I went to the nurses' station and tried to force them to give me the report. They didn't want to and kept saying I had to wait for the doctor to come back to give me the results directly. I wouldn't let up and went into lawyer-threatening mode. I rarely do this, but I am pretty good at it, so they relented and gave me the report.

Even though I knew what it was going to say, my heart sank when I read it. Kevin's cancer was back, and there was another brain tumor that was even larger than the one removed less than two months earlier. Plus there were "focal points" all over the rest of Kevin's brain, which meant that the tumor had spread everywhere. The doctor called me a few hours later and said he thought Kevin had maybe two to four months left. I knew he was wrong. I knew it would be much sooner.

CHAPTER 50

HEART-TO-HEART COMMUNICATION

Catherine

Needless to say, the entire writing with Kevin and Jocelyn had been intense, with the full gamut of emotions and resistance turned into surrender. I was most intrigued by Kevin's references to "heart-to-heart" communication. He said, "I'm not speaking from my grey matter, but from my heart, and it's strong and beating."

We assume that humans formulate their thoughts and ideas through their minds. Although there are hundreds of books and references to "speaking from the heart," Kevin seemed to say he was coming from a different place and formulating the conversation in a way he had never done before. He also commented that he was feeling stronger, more alive, and felt himself enlarging. I wondered whether his sensations and feelings were similar to experiences during meditation or prayer, when we quiet our thoughts and go to our heart to connect with the divine and our deeper self. We hope that with the mind silenced, even momentarily, we can create an open space to hear the still, quiet voice inside us.

What Kevin seemed to be alluding to transcended merely centering or grounding himself in his heart. It involved actually activating and connecting his heart to Jocelyn's. Perhaps his diminished brain function increased this heart-to-heart ability. It's estimated that somewhere between 20,000 to 50,000 thoughts go through our minds per day. Maybe when the mind's endless thoughts and worries abate, we truly can more easily connect with our deeper insights and truths.

Other than during the writings, Kevin's ability to communicate essentially didn't exist. From all appearances, he was unresponsive to touch and voice, but he sensed the whispers of Jocelyn's heart. Even more astonishing was how he heard within her what she couldn't even hear.

Many of us in challenging times find that our doubts, fears, and sense of helplessness give rise to greater confusion and despair. The negative voices in our heads can tend to grow louder and gain momentum. Kevin spoke of this kind of head versus heart battle within Jocelyn. Her head-based messages were desperate and intensified, given the unbearable realities she was facing. However, the heart-based truths within her that Kevin spoke about seemed to encompass acceptance, quiet strength, and comfort.

These examples don't just apply to Jocelyn in this profoundly sad situation. Many of us may think about and rail obsessively against unwanted circumstances or events in our lives, feeding ourselves "what if" and "if only" narratives. Our doubts, fears, and doom-and-gloom prophecies can sometimes, regardless of our efforts to rid ourselves of them, become self-fulfilling. Attempts to eradicate feelings can sometimes foster an even greater sense of discomfort, alienation, and helplessness. In our frenzy to deal with life's challenges, we can lose contact with our own heart and the essential truths within us.

Kevin said, "It's not Holy, it's Wholly Spirit, and that's where we are connecting through." Most likely he was referring to the heart, soul, or spirit within us that is unassailable in the face of life's difficulties and tragedies. I was reminded that our hearts are always whole in spirit, not only in times of great stress but also as we live each day. Our hearts are resonant places of love and connection. Whether it's the connection between the self and our heart, or heart-to-heart with another, it matters not. Love is a fluid connection.

Unconditional love is possible, but we must release our barriers wherever they reside: in our mind, our ego, or our sense of protectiveness or unworthiness. Kevin said, "Go to that place in your heart. No middle person—just you and me. Our hearts are one." This seemed to me to echo the essence of unconditional love as a true, loving connection within ourselves, with others, and with the divine.

CHAPTER 51

LOVE, FAITH, AND CHARACTER

Catherine

Most writings I do are only about twelve pages. The one on the UCLA patio was 68. As the session progressed, Jocelyn was transforming. This woman who was fiercely protective of Kevin, self-defended, and who chewed out the nurses was now more relaxed and accepting, even able to laugh.

Although Kevin was still going to die soon and Jocelyn was heartsick, her denial and resistance were waning. I was so grateful, as I always am whenever I do a writing. However, this was so much deeper. God had given a gift to Kevin, Jocelyn, and their family. Grace was able to enter and move into even this darkest of places. Through love and connection, Kevin found a way to bring light and wisdom to the desperate reality they were facing. His request to go to hospice would lighten the despair and the weight of caring for him that had awaited his family. Kevin's love, faith, and character inspired me.

In the span of a few hours, Jocelyn had let this difficult news penetrate. Kevin was dying and there was nothing she could do. She even allowed the nurse to put him back into bed. She expended her last battle cry on the nurses who had denied her the MRI report. From Kevin's room, we could hear Jocelyn arguing at the nurses' station. When she came back to the room, she looked like a dejected dog.

"The cancer is back," she announced. "It's everywhere—Kevin was right."

I think Vicky and I gave a collective gasp and sigh. Jocelyn seemed almost resigned and eerily calm. Since it was 4:30 p.m. and none of us had eaten all day, Jocelyn said, "The least I can do is buy you dinner before you head back."

We walked to her hotel, sat by the pool, ate, and had a great conversation. Jocelyn was chatty, fiercely bright, and funny. She seemed to need this non-medical, normal conversation of which she had been deprived for so long. She called her kids and told them she was taking Kevin to hospice instead of home. To her surprise, they weren't angry but relieved. It was a wise decision for all of them. We talked for a solid two hours. This was the longest she had been away from Kevin since they arrived in UCLA seven weeks ago. I assured her that she would be able to stay overnight at Serenity House. I sang their praises, having helped a friend pass away there a few months earlier.

Serenity House would be a blessing. We live in such a sanitized, death-aversive culture, and yet death is as natural as birth. Often in the face of death or a terminal illness, we want to pour all our love, care, and energy into what precious time remains. It's heartbreaking to be helpless and to watch someone suffer. Jocelyn's responses weren't unexpected or unusual. We are taught to believe that most things in life can be fixed or changed. When they can't, we may resort to anger, denial, or overcompensation. Yet there is a point when the dying process becomes unstoppable.

Medications can help ease a patient's physical pain, something for which we can be truly grateful. However, there is no treatment for a loved one's emotional pain, stress, fear, bewilderment, and sheer exhaustion. For them, these emotions can be overwhelming and intense. Faced with the undeniable process of death, we feel inept in terms of knowing how to support either others or ourselves. Our own discomfort can cause us to unwittingly distance ourselves from people, which often contributes further to the isolation and loss inherent in the dying process.

We don't need to face death alone. We can allow ourselves to be gently held and supported. Places like Serenity House, hospice services, and support groups are lifelines for people in their deepest hour of need. Kevin said in the first writing, "Death isn't a failure." He knew that Jocelyn saw it as a failure. In the heart-to-heart connection they now had, he also knew that she felt as if she was letting him down by not caring for him at home.

Like Jocelyn, many people in this situation feel that allowing essential care, help, and support from others is a sign they aren't being loving or are abdicating their responsibility. Sadly and tragically, the increasingly physical demands of care can and do impact our ability to be fully present for loved ones and ourselves. Serenity House would tend to Kevin and support Jocelyn and their children in this sacred transition. The dying process would be emotionally difficult, but it would be lovingly and naturally embraced and supported.

CHAPTER 52

LIVING AND LOVING
ROLE MODEL

Catherine

When we left for UCLA that morning, I did what I always do. I trusted, made myself available, and stepped into the wider stream of love and connection. Had Vicky and I not gone, in 24 hours Kevin would have returned home, where his family would have watched him slowly die. I told Jocelyn that Kevin deserved the right to spare his family having to go through this feeling alone and isolated. Just because he was dying, he shouldn't be denied the right to love and care for his family, but should be allowed to protect them with the same unwavering dedication and love they were showing him.

I was in awe that in just a few hours Jocelyn had gone from being stubbornly defensive to reluctantly accepting. When she finally called hospice, Kevin said, "We will let fate decide." Fate had spoken. He wasn't afraid, and he knew they would be together again. He had poignantly and beautifully expressed his love and gratitude throughout the writing. I reflected on one particular exchange:

My Wholly Spirit says thank you. Who could have thought in the last days of my life I'd really, really be able to be blessed with loving you more. No limit. I wish I could just sprout some wings here and now.

Kevin demonstrated how central love and faith can be, especially when we need them the most. For me that afternoon Kevin was a vibrant, loving role model. He embodied a welcoming, fearless receptivity as he approached his entry into this thing called death that we each must face.

CHAPTER 53

SERENITY HOUSE

Jocelyn

The ambulance came the next morning to take Kevin to Serenity House. As we were driving on the 101 freeway toward Santa Barbara, I was thinking of all the times we had traveled that road. You have to drive the 101 to get anywhere south of Santa Barbara, and we had taken that route many times to visit Kevin's parents in San Diego, to take the kids to Disneyland, or to get to Los Angeles International Airport when we were going on vacation.

Once we arrived at Serenity House, Kevin was wheeled into his room and put into the last bed he would ever sleep in. Even though I knew this was what he wanted, I was sad and disappointed for all of us that he would never be in our home again.

Serenity House is a beautiful place. The rooms look more like a high-end hotel than hospital rooms. They all have patios, and a lot of them have beautiful views of Santa Barbara and the Pacific Ocean. There are walking paths and trails all over the property. There is also a living room with a piano, plus a library. Their commercial kitchen makes delicious meals for patients and their families. If you were going to spend your last days away from home, I couldn't think of a more beautiful and peaceful setting.

Serenity House also offered so many other wonderful things. They had a volunteer group of singers who come into the patients' rooms to sing anything that they could want. I had them come, and they sang all of Kevin's favorite songs from the Beatles, James Taylor, and Eric Clapton. When they had finished, there wasn't a dry eye in the room.

Because Kevin was raised Catholic, they asked me if I wanted a priest to come and perform last rites. I had no idea whether Kevin would have wanted this, but I figured it couldn't hurt, so a priest came and administered this final ritual.

Serenity House also had a Reiki massage therapist on staff. Even though I didn't buy into that stuff, I thought that anything which might make Kevin more comfortable was worth it. When the therapist arrived, she ran her hands a few inches over Kevin and pronounced him ready. I told her she probably said that to everyone she worked with, just to make the family feel better. She said that in fact many people she works with die kicking and screaming. I knew that Kevin was ready, because he had told me so in the writing a few days before. But even if we hadn't had that writing, I knew he was ready because his faith in what was awaiting him was so strong.

It was me who wasn't ready.

CHAPTER 54

AN IRISH WAKE

Jocelyn

I had made a very short list of the people who I would allow to visit Kevin while he was at Serenity House. Santa Barbara is a small town. Word had gotten out within a day or two that he was there. Everyone who ever knew him wanted to come and say goodbye. I didn't want that.

Dying isn't a spectator sport, and I didn't want anyone except our family and a few close friends to see Kevin during his last days. Maybe that was selfish of me, but I felt fiercely protective of him. I was determined that his last days should be private, saved for the few people who were really important to him.

On our second day at Serenity House, some of our closest friends and family came by in the late afternoon. Someone brought several bottles of wine. Kevin loved a good bottle of wine, and so it seemed fitting that we all drank wine while spending what for most of them would be their last evening with him.

We opened the French doors to Kevin's room and wheeled his bed into the late afternoon sun. Everyone sat on the patio, and I sat with Kevin on his bed. We told funny Kevin stories, laughing and crying while we all sipped wine until the sun set. Kevin was Irish, so this was like an Irish wake—though he was still alive.

Kevin's hospice doctor came by and remarked that this was how it should be. When someone is dying, the way to send them off should be with them surrounded with loved ones, laughing and sharing stories of their lives together. I didn't want Kevin's last days to be filled with anxiety, and that evening was the perfect goodbye for him and our friends.

CHAPTER 55

DYING BEFORE MY EYES

Jocelyn

I was so relieved that we had taken Kevin to Serenity House. I had no idea how brutal it is to watch someone slowly die. Even if Kevin hadn't strong-armed me to get him there, I'm sure I would have taken him within a day or two. There was no way I could have gone through this at home. To say it was horrendous would be an understatement.

Since Kevin had pneumonia, every breath he took sounded like he was breathing under water. His breath didn't just rattle, it sounded like someone drowning, which he essentially was. His breathing became irregular to the point that he was only taking one breath every minute or so. I was watching the clock and timing each breath. If he took more than a minute without a breath, I shook him and yelled, "Breathe!" His heart rate was so slow, less than 20 beats a minute. He was dying before my eyes. There were so many times I wanted to call 911 and have him taken to the hospital to try and help him live a little longer, but I didn't. I didn't because I knew that wasn't what he wanted.

Just like at UCLA, I stayed with him around the clock. I slept in the bed with him, while our kids slept on the floor. The hospice folks were loving and supportive, but not in an in-your-face way, which I would have hated. They were just an accepting presence. His doctor, Michael Kearney, is one of the world leaders in palliative care. They knew, as we all did, that Kevin wasn't leaving this place alive.

It was all about comfort for the person dying, their family, and friends. I knew Kevin wasn't in any pain. He was on a continuous morphine drip that they kept increasing, and there was a pump we could push to add more every ten minutes. Needless to say, every nine minutes I started pushing the pump's button. I didn't want Kevin to be uncomfortable. Since he couldn't talk, the only indication of pain was if his brow was furrowed. Since he was unconscious anyway, I wanted him to be as unaware as possible about what was happening. Morphine seemed the best way to accomplish this.

While Catherine was at UCLA, she had offered to write for us again at Serenity House. I didn't imagine I would take her up on it. What was the point? Kevin was where he wanted to be, and I figured that her work was done. What was there left to say?

The day after our Irish wake on the patio, Catherine emailed me and said that if I changed my mind and wanted a writing, she was available. She didn't push, only made the offer, leaving it up to me to decide. Looking back on it, I think she felt Kevin wanted to talk to the kids before he died.

We left UCLA on August 30. It was now September 2, 2013, three days later. At this point, I figured Catherine knew more than I did. If she felt compelled to come, there must be more that Kevin wanted to say before he died. So I took her up on her offer and she came that evening.

CHAPTER 56

THE DIVINE'S WILL

Catherine

Serenity House was about as perfect a place as anyone could want for their final transition. Death isn't a sanitized, fearful, isolating and repellant process at Serenity House. Comfort and ease for patients and families are paramount. Kevin had told Jocelyn he was ready, and he had also readied her as best he could.

I was grateful to have been able to help Kevin and Jocelyn. In my own life, I've had personal experiences with the dying process, caring for my mother in the hospital, my close friend Dawn at Serenity House, and my sister-in-law Shelley who died in our home. I know time and space can feel altered and elongated. Clock time falls away, days and nights merge, and there is a profound shift in the energy. Strong feelings of reverence and sacredness become discernible, similar to being in a holy place or in moments of oneness in nature. There is a palpable sense of knowing that the dying person is ready to go, and also that you are ready to release them. With this acceptance of mortality, an inexplicable sense of peace comes. There is an overwhelming gratitude for sharing the dying person's life, along with a deeper appreciation for the gift of life itself.

The death process is paradoxical. In the face of death and loss, all of our pretenses and any barriers between us and our experiences, as well as between each other, become evident. We are given an opportunity for intimacy and to be exposed, so that we can be authentically present and connected. This depth of connection seldom happens in our daily lives. Those who attend to and support the dying as family members, friends, or health-care workers know that the dying process can be a "sacred space."

When we were still at UCLA, I had offered to do another writing. I emailed Jocelyn after a few days, again offering to come to Serenity House. "Yes, please!" she responded, warning me that the kids probably would be resistant and disbelieving. This was about Kevin and his family, not about me, so I had no agenda or expectation concerning the way they received me. God never sends me into a situation I'm not meant to be in.

Jocelyn met me in the Serenity House lobby and tried to prepare me for the onslaught. Her kids didn't know why I was coming. I was their Aunt Vicky's friend and I didn't know their parents. I told Jocelyn not to worry about me, assuring her that if the interchange became contentious, I would simply leave.

The children were present when I entered Kevin's room. In the few short days since I had seen him last, he had changed dramatically. His breathing was loud and irregular, fluid-filled and labored, and the death rattle was omnipresent. Despite the sound, which I knew all too well, he seemed pain-free and not in distress.

I sat in a chair next to Kevin's bed and briefly informed his children that I had facilitated two previous sessions with their dad. One of them was upset. Apparently Jocelyn had told them about the first writing, but not the second. "How could you? You promised you wouldn't do this again!"

"If I hadn't done that last writing, we'd be at home alone dealing with this," Jocelyn responded. "Being at hospice was what Kevin wanted. He didn't want us to go through this at home."

Jocelyn's child was incensed with her and proceeded to turn on me. "My dad is a Christian. He wouldn't want you to be doing this. I don't believe you can do this. It's not real. You shouldn't be here!"

I didn't take the hostility personally. To the contrary, I said, "Look, I know this is most unbelievable. I struggled myself when this began happening with me, but it's real and it's helpful. I'm a Christian too." The kids asked me how I knew I was sensing and connecting with God and their dad. It was a mini-inquisition, but I empathized with their concern for their father. I spent a good 30 minutes sharing the story of how this gift came to be. I explained that in the beginning I was reluctant and questioned that the source was truly God. But after hundreds of writings, I had no doubt that my gift was from God. There was no way I could know the information that was shared in a writing or any way to conjure up the miracles I had witnessed firsthand. More importantly, I told them the writings were always transformative, that they were both a blessing and a healing experience for the recipients.

Jocelyn, who had tried to calm the situation, finally said, "I asked Catherine to come here and this is happening. If you don't like it, then step outside because it's going to happen."

I got out my pen and paper. They asked me a few questions about the process, and then I began writing.

Hospice Writing

September 2, 2013

CHAPTER 57

LOVE YOU, DAD

The McIvers Family and Catherine

GOD: Welcome, the McIvers family. The aroma of your love fills the room. There is in this a vine of love in your family that can't be broken. In death's pruning, there is nothing it can take from us, for life has more to give beyond the grave. The spirit of love transcends the apparent separation, for in truth it is the place that has no separation. The heart that loves knows no boundary, for life has no barriers.

The aroma referred to in this introduction, it seemed to me, was love, and Kevin's family was the vine and the origin of this love. It also said death wouldn't separate them. God was reassuring them that they would remain connected after Kevin's death.

CHILD: Hi, Dad.

To protect the children's privacy, some portions of the writing, their comments and names have been removed at times.

186

KEVIN: You say "Hi, Dad," as if it's a phone call. This isn't a phone call. This is our time together and I need promises from each of you that this isn't going to come between you. I have no fear at all. God has called me and my moment to fall into his arms is close.

CHILD: What do you see? Do you see angels?

KEVIN: I don't see a different room or angels. I can't say anything more. There is a glorious bright light. Stop arguing.

The kids were bickering back and forth here about whether this was really him, and we laughed because he heard the bickering.

KEVIN: It feels good to hear you laugh. This is how I want it to be. Us. Just us, the same as always. Even Chris, from the interruption force, all testing and testy. I'll even take that. I want it to be normal. I want it to be us! Just like this, the same old us. Not the fights or complaining, because I want promises from all of you that you'll let it be as it always is. You have to be there for each other. I can't blow the whistle or send you to your corners.

CHILD: Love you, Dad.

CATHERINE: You know what he just said? Right now when you said that? He said:

KEVIN: You have to make this about the love you have for each other. Promise me that you will be about the love.

Catherine interrupted the writing here and said, "It starts working like that. It's a communication. I'm just still writing because the energy is so big. I'll read it to you when the energy slows down." She wrote for almost half an hour before she finally stopped and read it back. Catherine had to talk loudly to be heard over Kevin's labored breathing.

KEVIN: That love doesn't go out with me. It's inside me and inside each of us, and so it's love's promise. You need each other. Don't turn on Chris. He is hurting too. It's about showing him your tolerance, the understanding that you have capabilities and maturities that escape him. So be gentle with him above all. He is the fragile one—a porcupine but with a loving heart. So go gentle, go easy. Don't turn your anger on him, even though he provides a big red target.

Love, love, love. If I could hold you each in my arms—bring it in! I'm in your heart, and I will always be. So I need promises. Promises from all of you.

CHAPTER 58

INTO THE WATER

CHILD: Hey, Dad, can you hear me? I have some serious doubts about this. We know something you did at Bass Lake that was horribly embarrassing. It involved the boat we share with our neighbors. If you can, tell Catherine what you did with the boat. Tell her what happened because that would really help me believe this is you.

KEVIN: Into the water.

We went to Bass Lake every year with our great friends and neighbors, who we own a boat with. One year we went there before them, so we towed the boat with us. They normally towed it since they were the boat people and we weren't. Before we left home, we had taken the plug out of the back of the boat to dry it out. I was worried that Kevin would forget to put the plug back in. He assured me he wouldn't. Of course, he did. Once we got to Bass Lake, Kevin took the boat to the dock by our rental house and we left it there to go for dinner. During dinner, the thought struck me that maybe Kevin had forgotten to put the plug back in the boat. He wasn't sure whether he had, so we went to the dock and found that the boat had sunk to the bottom of the lake.

We had to call someone to get the boat out and fix it so that our vacation wasn't ruined. It was actually pretty funny at the time, even though it cost us more than the boat was worth to get it up and running in a single day.

There was no way that Catherine could have known what happened with the boat at Bass Lake. This was the turning point in the writing for the kids. They knew without a doubt that Catherine was connecting with Kevin, even though he was more dead than alive at this point.

Though I had no idea what the trick question meant, apparently the answer completely settled whether or not this was really Kevin. The recognition that their dad was speaking to them brought the children a tremendous sense of relief. The change was visible in their more-relaxed postures, facial expressions, and demeanor.

KEVIN: I'm not asking you to believe this is real, because you have to believe it in your heart. I'm not trying to convince you. The truth is, you'd never be convinced, and that's why I love you. You're smarter than smart and play stupid only when it suits you. You should believe what's in your heart, and it wouldn't be my expectation for you to do anything less. I'm not trying to be a model. As I always have, I'm trying to hold my family together.

The kids commented here that Catherine was writing really fast. I know it helped them believe what was happening. When she does a writing, she just writes as fast as she can, only pausing to read it when the inspiration has ceased.

CHAPTER 59

HOLD ONTO EACH OTHER

KEVIN: This isn't fixable. This isn't "Call in the Cavalry." Please respect that I saw my brother go, and I was changed. Why was I so convinced that being a good human being was so essential? It was my credo, but I decided it watching my brother go. It's about how you live, how you are with people, how you are an expression of goodness and are living goodness. I decided on that day that my life must count. I decided that I would make my life one that was for the both of us. I still got a little derailed along the way. We all do, and you will as well. Your mom will, and that's okay. But being that goodness, that's what matters.

When I met your mom, I was convinced I'd never get hooked up with a woman again. She came in with her way and handcuffed me. I was taken by her. I didn't want to be free. I want each of you to know that kind of love. I want you to know what it means to have someone who still loves you with every breath, even when you are a Mr. Potato Head. Though I wish you never had to go through something like this. I'm so sorry. I didn't get to choose, God did, and we have to respect him. We all live on God's time. My point is, we need to make that time matter and make the world better for those we love and those we don't even know. I wish you to know that to be your dad has been my greatest joy. Each one of you has brought me more moments and more depths of myself. I love you. I love you all!

> *Kevin was reaching his arm out at this point. I was surprised, because he hadn't moved in days. I asked him what he was reaching for.*

KEVIN: I'm reaching to say it's okay. It's all okay. I want us to be "us." And when we leave here, I want us to be "us."

CHILD: I love you, Dad.

KEVIN: And that love doesn't go away. It doesn't go away!

> *It was touching to hear this father share his values and where they had come from. Later I asked Jocelyn whether Kevin had ever talked about his brother's death and its impact on the man he became. She said she hadn't heard him speak about it much, and never about the influence his brother's death had on Kevin's life. I wondered whether Kevin was like so many of us who fail to really take the time to fully articulate, clarify, then share with those closest to us our life's purpose, values, and credos.*

KEVIN: Okay, so the promises now. You will hold onto each other and won't take it out on mom. She needs you, all of you. She plays like she is this tower of strength, but you know who was always there as her foundation. We leaned on each other, so now you need to lean on each other. I don't want to hear that there is any blame or judgment.

> *Our kids were talking back and forth, and over each other. Just the usual kid bickering.*

KEVIN: The bickering, it's all so normal. But it's what I want! Love is in every disgruntled utterance. Same ole, same ole. But I just don't want you to make your feelings an excuse to be mean, not to each other. Love is what you all are to me, and that's what you need to know.

CHAPTER 60

IT'S ALL LOVE

KEVIN: However this works, I'm grateful. I live in your hearts. I'm inside you, and you're inside me. I wanted so much to be with you for all those turning points. To see grandkids, to ride them on my knee. So I want you to know I will be doing this in spirit. I believe in God and Jesus and all the angels, saints, and powers that be. I will watch over you. I will love you. I will always listen, and I will try to guide you quietly.

I have the utmost confidence in each of you, in your abilities, and in your loving, kind ways. God's hand circles you and my whole family. I couldn't do this if I didn't know this. I am Wholly Spirit.

As he had done with Jocelyn at UCLA, Kevin was trying to pave the way for them to not blame God. He was reassuring them that though he would be physically gone, he would always be with them and had faith that God would be with them too. What Kevin expressed wasn't just his faith, but also a true knowing that let him face his death with grace, ease, and peace.

CHILD: Do you know how much longer you have?

KEVIN: It's closer now. And you, all of you, are wholly part of me! Into my Father's House I'm going, but I go as a father who has been blessed with you remarkable beings—and you, my wife. I promise you, I will never stop my love for you. My love goes on. I'm going around the bend, but I'll be waiting there.

CHILD TO
CATHERINE: I have a lot to say when you are done writing.

KEVIN: And even then you still wouldn't be quiet. That's why we loved you from the first word. I want it to be normal! Us to the last breath. Love, love, love, love, love, love! That's all I can tell you. It's all love! Don't think for one second that I left you.

CHILD: Love you, Dad!

KEVIN: And you say it, but really you don't have to, because I'm always feeling your love.

> *Then came a really funny moment. Just then, one of our kids "passed wind," really loudly. The other kid said, "Was that you?" and he answered, "No, it was Mom. Seriously, that wasn't me!"*

KEVIN: So it's normal! I asked for it and I got it.

> *Kevin was very polite. Even in this state, he was still directing traffic with his kids. After hearing what Kevin had said, the child who had been so hard on me at the beginning had now done a complete 180-degree turn.*

CHILD: I love you, Dad. Thanks for having me.

KEVIN: Thank you for being here.

> *Our youngest child Will was born when we were both older. We wanted him so badly. I had two miscarriages in trying to*

have him and almost gave up. We always told Will that we were so thankful we had him, and he would reply, "Thanks for having me."

KEVIN: I'm so glad we aren't at home. I want that house, our house, to be full of only good memories. This is just a little dark ending, too soon, to a bright and wondrous tale, all loving. So let it be that love! I am Wholly Spirit, and you are wholly me. We are wholly a family.

I love you! If I could gobble you up one by one, I would. I love you! Be there for each other. Be kind to each other. Mom will be fine. You all will in time. But I'm going to get my guardian angel wings. I think I'm guaranteed. This is God's grace, to be loved and loving. It's simply love. Love is the only recipe to life. It's not any more complicated than that. So feast, my sweeties. Love, love, love! Feast, my sweeties, and know my love is all about you.

Thank you for letting me live my promise to my brother that I'd use this life to live for both of us. But you know what I now know? He was my guardian angel. He brought all of you to me. And I know that if I hear a beep beep, it's him at the curb coming to get me—and that's okay. Because I love! I love! I love! I'm so grateful. We are always one heart beating, one love—my family.

GOD: Go with God.

After the writing was over, our kids were kind of stunned. While they were doubtful when the writing started, they weren't doubtful by the end. They knew that they had just had the last conversation with their father they would ever have.

I'd been at Serenity House for over two hours. The intensity upon my arrival had dissipated. Kevin had been able to share so much with his family in his final hours. I suspected he'd die soon now. Perhaps he had held on just to reassure them that they would all be okay.

Kevin also talked about his anticipation that his brother would greet him upon his death. Kevin was looking forward to that moment. In many writings, deceased people report being greeted by loved ones, and sometimes beloved pets.

CHAPTER 61

I Know It's Late

Catherine

Everyone was exhausted by the end of the writing. It had been tender, humorous, sad, open-hearted, and expansive. They had said their final goodbye. When closure happens, it can feel miraculous. People so often experience a softening and movement toward letting go after receiving these types of writings.

Since my husband had dropped me off at Serenity House, Jocelyn insisted on driving me home, which she said was the least she could do. Like at UCLA, her willingness to leave Kevin's side illustrated the renewed strength and confidence she seemed to receive from being able to connect with him.

Around 11:30 p.m., exhausted, I collapsed into bed. Wired from the evening, I tossed and turned. After midnight, out of the blue and without any solicitation on my part, I felt Kevin's energy again. He wasn't intrusive, but rather kind and gentle. Politely and apologetically, he conveyed, "I know it's late and I'm sorry to bother you. Can I impose on you one more time?"

It's extremely rare for someone who I've just connected with to come to me unsolicited to inspire me to write another message.

Despite my exhaustion, I got out of bed. I didn't trek downstairs to get my usual writing paper. Instead, I used a yellow legal pad that was next to my bed. "How appropriate," I thought, "given that Kevin and Jocelyn were both lawyers." I noted the date and the time (12:34 a.m.) The alignment of 1234 struck me. "Ready, set, go" maybe?

At 2:06 a.m. and 17 pages later, I put down the pen. When I climbed back into bed, I had no problem falling asleep. Despite the sadness this family was facing, I knew an abiding love and grace surrounded them.

CHAPTER 62

KEVIN WROTE YOU A LOVE LETTER

Jocelyn

The morning after Catherine's writing at Serenity House with our family, she called me and told me that after she got home, Kevin came to her and asked her to send me a message. I didn't know at the time that she sometimes received unsolicited requests from a deceased person, asking her to relay a message. She told me that she had never received an unsolicited message from someone who was still alive. I asked her what the message was. I thought it would be brief, such as to tell me that Kevin was happy the kids had been able to have a conversation with him before he died. She said it wasn't a brief message. She said, "Kevin wrote you a love letter."

She emailed me the letter right away. When I was alone with Kevin in his room, I read it out loud. Of course, I cried the whole way through it. It was the most beautiful thing anyone had ever said to me. Of all the writings up to this point, and all the ones yet to come, this one has always been my favorite.

Love Letter Writing

September 3, 2013

CHAPTER 63

TRUE NORTH

Kevin and Catherine

GOD: Welcome, Jocelyn. When the road begins to change and all that has been traveled before seems distant in memory, turn within to the roadmap of the heart, which has etched into it each moment with great exuberance a life well lived. For within the journey, the compass of love has always guided the way. Two poles have found the magnetism that helped the other call themselves to True North. This is within you, though it be in this hollow time of pouring out. All spent from the final miles of the journey, you are called into labor, from which you will be lifted and received in sweet relief. What appears distant or even disappearing can never be taken or stretched to a vanishing point unseen. For True North lives on, always present. The magnetic pull that called you to sense self in relationship hasn't abated. Through the alchemy of physical life transformed to spirit unended, your spirit and relationship is distilled into this new and unfamiliar holding. Allow True North to direct you. Your center, your union, your relationship changed—yes. But the journey isn't finished. Soul-to-soul, heart-to-heart, love-to-love, it is eternal and infinite.

With such stunningly beautiful metaphors, it's easy to let the words wash over you, so much so that you fail to take in their deeper meaning. In loss, the road does change, and the landscape of our lives can be severely and irrevocably altered. Each death is uniquely individual. For those who haven't directly witnessed the dying process, there comes a time when your prayers to let the dying person live change into prayers to let them die gently and be free. Being lovingly present and accompanying someone to the point of physical death is sacred. God reminds us all "to turn within, to the roadmap of the heart" and that "the compass love" will always guide us. What a relief that we are all innately designed for even this part of the human experience.

Love is an ever-present compass in our journeys, whether we are on a mountaintop or in a valley in our lives. We are invited to look beyond our usual compass of the mind and intellect as our means of traversing our experiences. What a gift to expand our awareness and ourselves to include the heart that guides us and has its own knowing and attuning.

"True North" and the heart are offered as essential ingredients to set our focus, knowing, and direction. Just as we can see the needle on a compass move to reveal unseen magnetic forces, so it is with love and connection. The magnitude of love and connection isn't readily discernible, nor can their strength be measured by our five senses alone. Love and connection are real, powerful, and steadfast sources of our heart's direct experience on this journey called life.

Life is the journey, but death isn't the final destination. Nor does the journey itself end at death. For indeed, though we may question what lies beyond death's shore, we can trust that the journey continues. We don't fall into an abyss of nothingness at the edge of our physical life. Each loving experience and exuberant moment we have lived is etched upon our heart.

It turns out that True North is different from what we commonly think of as magnetic North. Wasn't this what God was really saying? Regardless of our positioning in the journey, either in our physical life or our celestial, heavenly, or soul realm, we can still be guided by our love compass. Even in death, those who have been guiding and loving forces of connection and direction don't stop being our True North. The journey continues soul-to-soul, heart-to-heart, love-to-love, ever eternal and infinite.

CHAPTER 64

MY SWEET GIRL

KEVIN: Oh my sweet girl, this evening was so necessary and it had to be about the kids. It was important to leave them with the sense that I hadn't left without saying, "I love you." I know you understood how important and necessary it was. It isn't even about belief or disbelief. It was tough, with the ultimate Doberman at the gate defending anyone who would dare trespass. I admire you for holding up and not wavering to let what I had to say be heard.

I still do not understand how this is possible, but I have no worries that it's anything but of light, God, and a blessing to all of us. But I couldn't use that precious time to say what I needed to say to you—it had to be for them. I'm glad Christopher didn't derail the connection tonight. Catherine is kind enough to come and walk into the craziness that is "us" to do this thing she is able to do, and for that I'm grateful.

I hope you understand it was important for me to reiterate how fragile Chris is and how gentle you all need to be with him. He will take my passing the hardest. He has always struggled with feeling different, misunderstood, singled out—the list goes on. He was our baby and maybe we just loved him unrestrained, or maybe he was always so sensitive. He is easily overwhelmed.

I know we have tossed all the possibilities over and over in our minds, in our debates, in our reactions, as attempts at distraction, bribes, and protection. But he needs the gentleness, the understanding, because he is with only one wing. He feels so damaged and doesn't even understand how to begin to control himself, so be gentle.

Don't allow him to abuse you, so it's not turning a blind eye. You have to remain vigilant, but remember that he is the most fragile and anger is his way to try to protect himself. His bravado is all a big farce for the three-year-old who is scared and lonely. We never left him, but in his heart he feels abandoned. My passing will even further exacerbate his feelings of abandonment and alienation. I know we together could barely weather his antics, but I fear in the wake of my passing he will only escalate them.

I don't tell you this to worry you, but to reiterate how important it is for you to get support for yourself and Will—not simply to think you can handle it or be unaffected. You don't have immunity where Chris is concerned, so you will have to not pretend. You have to not retaliate as others will, but be gentle, but not a doormat in the process. We always navigated the Chris waters together. While I'll try my very best to be there as your protector and guardian, I'm not sure how all that works yet, so don't say yes to abuse. Set your boundaries and keep them. I'm not in a position to judge you. If it turns abusive, then do what you must. But as he tantrums, see him as the scared three-year-old that has wet his pants. I do believe in time he will straighten up. I have to believe this—and if I am in a position to bring a real remedy to the situation, I will. You know I will.

Will, oh he is a snuggle bundle, the one that just was always easy, and so easy to love. A chance for us to just feel that it was possible to have a child who wasn't always bringing a level of complication and complexity. He is fiercely bright like you. But he hasn't had in the shadow of Chris ever exercised a need for any extra attention or capabilities. He was born easy because our family system couldn't handle one more high maintenance child, and that's okay. His ability to cope and get through this unchanged will be directly related to how well you allow yourself to do what's necessary to mourn, grieve, and let yourself feel the full impact of the disabling totality of your and our world being upended.

You can't outthink this. No amount of muscle or intellect is going to let you outrun it. So please do yourself—and most importantly for Will's sake—a favor, and utilize all that's available to support you. I can hear that grumbling, but Will is your little empath. And if you don't allow some processing of this, you'll box it up. It will be Will who will have to carry that box within himself for you the rest of his life, and that's not fair. That isn't what either of us wants for him. He needs to know you are letting yourself be taken care of, that it's not his job. Not that you ask this of him. It's his way. He tries so hard to be a good boy and take care of everyone. He is a good boy, but it's not his job. But when I pass, he will feel he has to do something to make it better for everybody, and of course he won't be able to.

So please my love, you need to take care of yourself. Don't try to outmuscle this. Allow yourself to crumble. You won't break—I know you. God in his divine wisdom must have known that I couldn't have been the one to let you go before me. I can wax poetic all I want to, but we both know you have always been the brains and the brawn of the McIvers' operation.

CHAPTER 65

NO MEASURE OR CEILING

KEVIN: Now for you, and what I couldn't and didn't want to say in front of our kids. I have loved you from the first moment our eyes locked. I say locked, because it really felt like that—that I was a goner, immediately and completely. You are the most passionate person I've ever known in all senses of the word and expressions. The pleasure you have brought me in our lives together has no measure or ceiling. We were and are equals in the truest sense of that meaning. There is no one else who I respect more, nor has there ever been. Your mind can outmatch anyone, and the funny and amazing part is you don't even recognize how extraordinary you are. It's just you being you, and what seems basic and obvious and a no-brainer to you would take a mastermind a while to compose and compute.

And your humor, oh my goodness. If we were to do the math on how many years of this slowly eroding lifetime I have spent laughing, with a dumb irrepressible smile on my face, well I'd have to say at least 25% of the time. And again, it was just you being you. It was never forced or contrived. It was just your humorous ways of seeing and saying. You could charm a snake with your wit and your charisma, and I've witnessed innumerable instances of this. Last word Annie, and you don't even know you have been bitten! Oh my, you aren't simply schooled and you aren't simply talented, my sweet wife. You are the quintessential whole package.

This brings me to a little footnote, but a necessary inclusion. In a time down the road, in a different and lighter place, you must give yourself a full life again. By full I mean you have a lot of life and years left. So, I'm not trying to be indelicate, but I want you to reengage life and love fully again. I don't want you to stop being vital and alive because I'm no longer there. I want you to love, explore, and express again whenever you feel that connection. Because I'm dead doesn't mean you have to die as well. I won't belabor this, but please understand, I don't need a celibate widow.

You have been my partner in all things. You and I grew up and fumbled through all of it together, and we did a damn good job most of the time. We have built a life together and a family together. We have flourished. We have surpassed and lived out even dreams we didn't know we had for ourselves.

How I would have loved to have had the time to take the trips we planned—to go see it, be it, enjoy it. I'm not saying this with the taste of regret though, so don't misunderstand me. With this deterioration coming on so quickly, I don't know how much I would have been able to fully enjoy it. It's possible that this impending growth would have overshadowed those things even if we had done them.

CHAPTER 66

GRATEFUL

KEVIN: So I have no regrets. To go into this passing without regrets, well I can't tell you how grateful I am to you, because you were always there. We walked it through together. To think and live ahead, without knowing that it would afford me in this time now—to not have to look back with any thought for where I misstepped or for a laundry list of undone or misdone things. I'm grateful to God for all of it, so grateful and grace-filled.

That Wholly Spirit wasn't some newfound language I picked up in my explorations. It's a reality I'm beholding from God's glory, and for me it's been surprising and exhilarating. For a guy who seems to have little to nothing going on upstairs, I've received a preview of the kingdom of heaven, and I say it's all good. It's better than good, it's amazing.

God gave me this life to do something with, to make my life a statement, to help my fellow man and woman. I think I've tried to do this in small, quiet, and humble ways. I'm grateful for that opportunity and every other opportunity God has given to inspire me and let me be a source of inspiration, comfort, or aid to another.

You haven't always agreed with me. In fact you sometimes laughed at my spiritual fervor. But it's saved me, and I pray others too from time to time. I'll miss my buddy and our deep conversations. Every spiritual quester needs a companion, and in God's divine providence I got that as well. I hope he can keep supporting you in small ways as well.

For my part, I would ask you to refrain from blaming God for this. I'm not asking for conversion, I'm just asking you to soften up from complete conviction and criminalization. Death is, it turns out, a very natural state of affairs.

Love is your religion whether you know it or not. I've always known it and seen it that way about you. I appreciate how you never denied me to seek out and participate in all the ways I felt God was leading and inviting me. You have always given me room to be all of myself, and I believe I also have given that to you. I think that was a part of our success as a couple—and, of course, being good in the sack. Had to put that in there to make you laugh!

We love each other and that love only rarely felt stagnant. We kept growing ourselves and our relationship. I never, ever wanted to be anywhere else than with you. After all our years, that's an unbelievable but deeply true statement.

I'm so sorry that you feel like you have been robbed, really because you probably can say that too. Here we are, I'm this skeletal lifeless form of my former self, lying in a bed, awaiting a passing. Thank you. Thank you for allowing my strong, firm-arm tactics the other day. Thank you for honoring my wishes and not bringing the memories of my last days to eclipse all the memories of life, laughter, tears, joys, and everything in between that happened in our house. I want you to go home and have it feel like home, like a sanctuary that holds love and support. Thank you for letting me love you as I wished to.

I didn't want you to think I overlooked you or hurried past you tonight. It was a time and place call, and I knew that what is between us could never really be conveyed. Your heart and mine are one, and you need look no further than your own heart to know I'm there. I don't know how it will be when I finally pass. I'm believing it's beyond my conception—that the real truth won't be known until it has happened. I'm not afraid. I'm not in pain. I'm not worried. There is a calm peace—that is what I'm soaking in.

If there be anything you need, know I'm doing all that I can to be with you, that my heart and your heart are one. Search your heart and you will find me there.

I must let this lady go to bed. She has been so kind to help our family. If there is such a thing as an angel on earth, then I think she needs a commendation.

I love you now, always, and forever, to galaxies yet to be discovered.

Love, your forever Kev.

CHAPTER 67

LOVE AND APPRECIATION

Catherine

The unsolicited writing session would turn out to be my last before Kevin died. Though the love letter was addressed to Jocelyn, Kevin's words are true for all of us. It isn't only about dying, but living out loud and intentionally every day. Clearly the number of years we live doesn't mandate or equate to the value or meaning of our experiences. Tragically for Jocelyn and her family, "living" would soon entail finding a way to live their lives without Kevin. We all experience loss, be it the death of a loved one, a failed relationship or job, a lost treasured possession, or the loss of a concept we hold as our identity. Despite these losses, our intrinsic capacity for love and connection remains strong.

Love and connection are powerful, unshakeable pillars of strength that help us live through even the worst of experiences. Even in the deepest trenches of life's challenges, people, events, and insights can unexpectedly offer wisdom, grace, and support. Unfortunately, there is a human tendency to protect, withdraw, and isolate ourselves in situations of overwhelming stress and pain. In times of sadness and loss, we may forget that our greatest resource and sense of aliveness is love and the connection it engenders. In times of pain, we can initially and reflexively choose the polarizing lens of darkness over light to view the experience. However, this tendency may obscure our ability to see and call upon our heart and spirit as valuable sources of discernment, wisdom and courage.

Life's regrets can be eased or eliminated by living in alignment with the higher values of love, faith, and service. Being grateful for all aspects of life, with its experiences and opportunities for growth and transformation, can yield incalculable treasures and returns.

We think people know how we feel about them. We take others and ourselves for granted. All of the richness, details, and nuances of love and connection are often reduced to "Love you," "Thanks a million," or pet nicknames. Kevin knew the importance of not dying without his love being clearly expressed. At Serenity House, he poured out a last goodbye to his family. He spoke of Jocelyn's passion, superior intellect, humor, and their equal partnership. She told me later that of course she knew he loved her, but she had no idea of the depth or details he shared. While the essence and awareness of Kevin's love were always her reality, his detailed sharing allowed that love itself to expand and be more deeply felt and embraced.

Thankfully, many of us make it a habit to express our love, caring, and appreciation towards others. On his deathbed, Kevin was given an opportunity to convey his love and gratitude, and we can do the same every day. We don't have to wait for death or loss in order to express our love. Some people have the gift of self-expression; others may find it difficult or embarrassing. Regardless, our expressions can be humorous, profound, or just a natural extension of the bond we share with another.

Sometimes even when the love is expressed, we can resist allowing ourselves to be open to receive it and believe it. Sadly we can fall prey to being "love deflectors" by minimizing, discounting, or rejecting positive messages. If we lack a positive self-concept and self-appreciation, we may use self-critique and judgment of being unworthy or unlovable as barriers to fully embracing ourselves and letting love in.

Even as romantic and demonstrative as Jocelyn says Kevin was, she said she didn't know all the "whys" of his feelings. Being complete when sharing and expressing doesn't have to involve sweet words, but may just involve including more specifics. It can be as simple as expanding on things like Kevin did in his gratitude for the laughter, by including the mention of the "dumb irrepressible smile" Jocelyn put on his face. It doesn't matter how eloquently or profoundly we say it, the bottom line is that we shouldn't wait to tell people just how and why we love them. Expressing love and gratitude is a precious gift of the heart that not only opens us up in the contemplation and articulation, but also can open up the heart of the other exponentially. Love and gratitude are key ingredients to a full and meaningful experience of connection in relationships and within oneself.

CHAPTER 68

WITHOUT ANGER OR REGRET

Catherine

Throughout the writings, the role Kevin's spiritual foundation served for him is apparent. He had loved deeply and dedicated his life to being of service to others. To be without regret or anger in the final days of his life signified how fully he had lived. He said he didn't have to look back with any thought of where he had misstepped or compile a laundry list of undone or misdone deeds.

What an illustration of living in accordance with one's values, purpose, and faith. What a powerful reminder to be in the driver's seat of one's own life, rather than dwelling on what could or should have been—not simply living with intentionality alone, but also amplifying and grounding our experiences in gratitude. I didn't know Kevin the man, but those who did assure me he embodied these principles of goodness, service, and trying to make a difference in the lives of others.

Kevin beseeched Jocelyn not to blame God and reminded her that love was her religion. Kevin well knew how sour Jocelyn already was on religion or faith, as well as on the possibility of receiving grace. If God existed, where was he and why was he making Kevin suffer and die? Jocelyn blamed God for abandoning Kevin and taking him from her and his family.

In times of loss, desperation, or confusion, our faith and connection to the divine can be a source of great solace and comfort. Kevin knew Jocelyn's anger and pain would only widen this divide between her and God, thereby further eliminating any chance of softening and helping her to accept this incomprehensible loss.

Kevin had no regrets or anger and wanted this for Jocelyn and his family. He knew that after his death they would be angry and devastated, but he also trusted in the power of love and connection. In all the writings, Kevin points Jocelyn toward focusing on the love and connection they shared, rather than becoming more embittered, blaming, and distancing herself from God. He wanted her to experience the loving power, protectiveness, and strength his faith had given him.

CHAPTER 69

MORE ESSENTIAL QUESTIONS

Catherine

In many writings Kevin consistently admonished Jocelyn to take care of herself. It's easy to focus our attention, energy, and caring so much on others who we perceive as more vulnerable or in pain, with the result that we become unconscious of our own needs and suffering. When caring for others is out of balance, we can abdicate responsibility to be kind and caring towards ourselves. Regardless of the situation, each of us deserves love, patience, and understanding. Kevin implored Jocelyn to gently care for herself and not close off her heart.

Surely if Kevin could have stayed and cared for his family, he would have. But we are all mortal beings. It isn't a question of whether our physical body dies. The more essential questions arise every second of our existence in all our choices and actions, those that are significant as well as those that are seemingly insignificant. The most central considerations are the what, when, where, why, and how of our expressions, creations, offerings, love, and connections. Our choices and actions don't merely indicate our priorities or focus of our energy. They combine to reveal our values, deeper nature, and essence. The paramount power and value lie in how we live, behave, and embody ourselves in all aspects of our lives. We shouldn't wait until our physical clock has wound down to fully inhabit and embrace these precious lives we are given. Nor should we await and use the shadow of death as the only real impetus to examine and transform our lives and ourselves.

We might all do well to actively engage with our life and ourselves by asking some key questions on a regular basis. How fully am I living in all the various dimensions of my life and self-expression? Is my behavior aligned and in harmony with my values? Do I feel and experience my intrinsic and loving essence? Do I show up in my life with a willingness to reveal, express, and embrace all that I am? Do I feel an authentic connection with my spirit, others, and myself?

These are only a few questions we can ask ourselves. Trusting that our heart knows how to articulate the particular questions that are most meaningful to us, we can allow time and space for the answers to arise. Actually listening and honestly contemplating whether we need to change our thinking, behavior, or actions is crucial. All of us determine how we will open and live these priceless gifts of life with which we have been entrusted.

CHAPTER 70

WHAT REALLY MATTERS

Catherine

As Kevin reminds us all, at the end of life it's love and connection that really matter. It was a soliloquy of sorts, though not hastily thought out and only lived into the remaining days before his death. Kevin purposefully set this in motion, in both form and experience each day he lived, loved, and connected with himself, others, and the divine. In the writings, he stated why he lived the way he did, his motivation, values, and profound gratitude for the love and gift of his life.

We all die, of course, but it's how we live that comprises the quality of who we are and the legacy we leave behind. Don't wait a moment longer to become the fullness of who you are created and given the opportunity to be. In the final analysis and transition through death's door, this person, this life, this infinite individual expression we each are goes with us. Although our bodies die, our love and connections, and our imprint on others, ourselves, and our world continue and are infinite.

Kevin's family would carry those memories of him tightly sewn into their minds and hearts. Though he seemed not to know when the hour of his final passage would arrive, he reiterated the power of their connection and vowed Jocelyn and he would remain as one. She only had to look inside her heart to find him. In the stifling absence that follows losing someone, it's easy to get sucked into and be consumed by the vast void left behind. We can remember in those sad times that our loved ones are always with us, always available to ease our grief and despair. The unbounded love we share and have for those we care about is rooted within us. We are reminded to call upon this love that is invincible, strong, and heroically present as a source to carry us through our grief and devastation.

Kevin died soon after the last hospice writing. He left behind a lot of family members, friends, and colleagues, and others he may have touched without ever knowing. Despite his death, Kevin's loving and spirit-filled imprint remains with all of them. The last lines Kevin shared with Jocelyn were:

> I love you now, always, and forever, to galaxies yet to be discovered.
>
> Love, your forever Kev.

In my own small speck of this universe, I am eternally grateful for the love and wisdom that come my way. Love is ever-present. Love is now, always, and forever. Love is infinite in all realms, seen and unseen. I believe this love and its transformational power begin within each of us and never end.

CHAPTER 71

KEVIN WAS GONE

Jocelyn

Kevin died four days after the Love Letter Writing. A moment after he took his last breath, his eyes flew wide open and he let out a surprised gasp. He had a look of awe and pure joy on his face. He hadn't opened his eyes in days and hadn't been able to open his right eye in weeks. I was so glad the stitches had been removed from that eye so he could fully see what I couldn't. That was the last time I ever looked into his eyes.

Before we left UCLA, I asked the neuro-oncologist whether donating Kevin's brain for research would help them find a cure for this horrendous disease. He said it would, because UCLA had all of Kevin's MRIs from the beginning of his disease until the end. They also had tissue samples from each of Kevin's surgeries and would be able to look back at the disease's progression. I knew Kevin would want to do whatever he could to prevent another family from going through this horrible ordeal. Literally, it was a no-brainer.

The hospice nurse dressed Kevin in his favorite jeans and a surfing T-shirt which one of our kids had given him for a

Christmas present years before. I took off his wedding ring and put it on my ring finger next to my wedding band. UCLA staff came to Santa Barbara and took him away.

Kevin was gone.

CHAPTER 72

TOTALLY EMPTY

Jocelyn

I don't think I have ever felt as lonely or alone as I did going home from hospice after they took Kevin away. I walked into our home and was overwhelmed with an unfathomable sadness. I remember standing in the front doorway and looking into the living room where we had spent countless evenings together. I walked down the hallway to our bedroom, which was empty because my sister had moved everything out to accommodate the hospital bed and medical equipment we had planned to use.

The empty bedroom seemed fitting because I felt empty. Beyond empty. I was emotionally and physically spent. I felt like I had been sprinting a marathon for the last two months and had just crossed the finish line. Usually when you cross a finish line, it's because you've accomplished something. You've won something. But for me, crossing the finish line just felt like that—finished.

I wandered around the house feeling bereft. There was nothing to do. Sure, the table was piled high with mail, there were groceries to buy, laundry to do, and most importantly children to console. But I had spent every moment of the last two months focused on Kevin, and now there was no Kevin. I felt I had lost not just the battle, but the war. I thought to myself, what do I do now? There was nothing left to fight for. The most important person in my life was gone. I was alone with a pile of mail, a bigger pile of laundry, an empty bedroom, and an empty heart.

After our kids had gone to bed, I sat on the couch in Kevin's favorite spot and poured myself a glass of red wine. I don't like red wine and prefer beer, but Kevin liked it. I had bought a really nice bottle before we went to UCLA, thinking that after we got home from his surgery he could enjoy it while we planned on tackling all the things on his bucket list. Now I was drinking it on my own, not really looking at the TV, and wondering what in hell I was going to do next. "Next" as in the next five minutes, and "next" as in the next five years.

I couldn't get the Love Letter Writing out of my mind because it was really the last thing Kevin said to me while he was alive. I decided to write a letter as well. Not really to him, but rather about him. So I went to his computer and wrote a letter to Kevin to send off into the cosmos. I'm not really sure why I did it, I just felt compelled.

A week or so later, my mother asked whether I planned on putting an obituary in the local newspaper. I hate those kinds of things and didn't want to sum up Kevin's life in terms of where he was born, what he did in his life, and so on. Instead, I decided to use that letter.

CHAPTER 73

KEVIN THOMAS McIVERS
9/28/53–9/7/13
A LIFE WELL LIVED

Dear Kevin,

I miss you so much. I am heartbroken that you are gone.

Anyone who knew you loved you. You had qualities all of us wanted but few of us possessed. You lived your life with joy and laughter and love for your family and friends.

You loved your work. Being a mediator suited you perfectly. You felt it was a calling, not a career. You wanted to help people work through what was often one of the most difficult times of their lives.

People who came to you in times of trouble felt like you really heard them, understood them, and wanted to help them. At the end of the day, you made most people's lives better. Not a lot of us can say that.

There were sides to you most people didn't know. You loved to surf. You loved music and to play the guitar (you even took weekly lessons). You liked Pinot Noir wine and would often wander to a neighbor's house with a bottle to share. You wore dress shirts on Sunday, just because it was Sunday. You were always reading a spiritual book. You would snack on cheese and dark chocolate. You watched political TV every night. You loved to play basketball.

There were things you never got to do but always wanted to do. You wanted to surf in Fiji. You wanted to take a Missions trip. You wanted to travel to Israel and visit the Holy Land. You wanted to see your children get married and have families of their own.

Kevin, you had a life cut short, but a life well lived. Not many people can say that.

From all of us who were blessed enough to have known you, thank you for sharing yourself. We are enriched beyond measure.

Love you always,

Jocelyn

CHAPTER 74

A BLUR

Jocelyn

The weeks following Kevin's death were a blur. I think we were all suffering from post-traumatic stress. Not from his death, which of course was devastating, but more from the two months before, during the period from when he underwent surgery to when he died.

I hadn't felt able to take a deep breath or have a calm thought since he was re-diagnosed. Now I had all the time in the world just to think and breathe. I rehashed everything over in my mind. Did we make the right decision in going forward with the second brain surgery? Did I make the right choices, dozens of times, from his first surgery until he died? Could I have done anything differently that would have changed the outcome? Did he suffer? Is he okay, wherever he is? Does he know what's happening with me and our children? If he does, does he think I'm making the right decisions now?

Being alone with my thoughts was my worst enemy. I was panicked, exhausted, overwhelmed. How was I ever going to be able to function? I had a job to get back to, a 13-year-old son who had just lost his father, and an adult child with struggles of his own.

The phone never stopped ringing. Everyone who knew Kevin called or emailed to tell me how sorry they were. At first I answered the phone, but then I stopped. I couldn't stand another person telling me that it was God's will, that Kevin was in a better place, or some other placating bullshit that just made me madder and madder at God. More than once, I had to hear the "God needed another angel so much that he couldn't wait, which is why he took Kevin" explanation for why my husband had died. The first few times I heard this, I mumbled something like, "Yeah, you're right." Of course, I didn't believe that. I just wanted to get the insensitive yet well-meaning asshole off the phone. If there was a God, you mean to tell me that in the millions of years that humans have inhabited the earth, he didn't have enough angels and needed one more?

The third time someone started in with that tripe, I'd had enough. "You've got to be fucking kidding me! Is that what you really think?" I blurted out and hung up the phone. After that I stopped answering my phone and changed my voicemail message to say, "Hi, this is Joc, you can leave me a message, but I probably won't call you back." Not a day later, I received an irate call from my mother who had heard about my voicemail message and demanded I change it. I refused. I was done talking to people who wanted to tell me there was a good reason for Kevin's death. There wasn't a good reason. There never is a good reason.

Then the cards of condolences started coming in. My mailbox was full of them. I opened the first few then stopped. They were all filled with platitudes about God and everlasting life. Although I was grateful that so many people loved Kevin, reading their words of sadness just made me sadder. I couldn't take it, so I stopped opening them. I still have a shoebox filled with unopened cards.

I was also given several books about heaven being real. I probably got ten copies of *Proof of Heaven* and *Heaven is for Real*. I know that people were just trying to make us feel better, but when you are in those early stages of grief, nothing helps. I never read any of those books. They all went to Goodwill.

I know that people don't really know what to say under these circumstances. When they say, "I know how you feel," they really don't. Not unless they have lost a husband or—in our children's case—a father when that person was still relatively young. Nobody can really know how you feel. When they say, "I'm sorry for your loss," which I'm sure they are, they are most likely thinking, "I'm glad it's you, not me."

Not wanting to hear any of these sentiments or have people try to hug me and rub my back, I simply stopped leaving the house. Except for a few close friends and family who had lived through the last few months with me, I shut myself off from everyone and everything. It felt safer to be holed up alone in the house with our kids.

CHAPTER 75

LIFE DOES GO ON

Jocelyn

B ut life does go on. Even if you don't want it to, it does. There are groceries to buy, laundry to do, bills to pay, pets to feed, etc. While you feel your world has stopped, the world around you hasn't. All the problems that were there before Kevin died were still there, but they felt multiplied because now I was handling them alone.

Our oldest son's drug addiction was worse than ever. We had to install a security system to keep him out of the house when we weren't there. He was suffering over Kevin's death just as much as we were, and the loss made him spiral deeper into despair. We all wanted to help him, but there was nothing we could do except protect ourselves from the fallout of his addiction. I was more worried about him than anything else at that point. I had just lost Kevin and I felt there was a real possibility our son would be next. Even if Kevin hadn't died, our lives at home were anything but peaceful.

About a month after Kevin died, I decided that our youngest son Will should return to school. He was in eighth grade. Staying home watching *The Office* reruns for a month wasn't helping him get his life back on track. Plus the stress of his brother's addiction made being at home worse. He needed some normalcy. Though he didn't want to go back to school, we all had to start living life again, even if we felt we were merely going through the motions or faking it.

Before Kevin's cancer returned, I was working on a murder case and needed to get back to it. I had put it off as long as I could. People with some serious life-altering issues were counting on me to get back in the game. So I returned to work, Will resumed his schooling, and all the while our oldest son was living in his truck and fishing aluminum cans out of trashcans to support his addiction.

Every day I wondered whether Kevin was okay. Where was he? Did his total existence end with his life? Was he with us, watching us? Did he know what we were all going through? Could he do anything to help our oldest son?

I know he believed he was going to a better place, but did he? I had to find out.

I was apprehensive about calling Catherine and asking her to do another writing so I could attempt to talk to Kevin. I didn't know whether she would be willing to do it or whether Kevin would even show up. As she had told me previously, she can't predict what's going to happen. If there was a chance it was going to be a total bust, I wasn't sure I wanted to try. In my mind it would be better to not know than to try, then find out I was unable to connect. Sometimes not knowing is better than just "no."

Catherine and I had kept in contact since the first writing. This contact had become more frequent and I felt like we were becoming friends. We were similar in many ways. I wished at the time that we had become friends through the normal channels—that it wasn't Kevin's illness and death that had put us on each other's radar. You want friendships to be on an equal footing, not based on the fact that one person has something the other wants. This was all the more reason I was apprehensive of asking Catherine to do a writing. She had already done so much for me and our family. She never asked for a dime and had gone out of her way several times to do, as she put it, "God's work." I didn't want to take advantage of her and really debated whether to ask her.

Of course, once I started thinking about being able to talk to Kevin again, it was all I could think about. I decided to suck it up and ask Catherine if she would do another writing. "Of course," she instantly responded, showing no hesitation whatever. Even though it had only been a little over a month since Kevin died, it felt like years. There were so many things I wanted to talk over with him. I had so many questions to ask and so much reassurance I needed.

We set up to meet within a few days. This time I went to her house, which I hadn't done until now. It struck me as funny that before we started, she lit candles. I couldn't help but smile to myself, because when she came to UCLA to do the writing, I was wondering whether candles were involved.

CHAPTER 76

YOUR ESSENCE REMAINS

Catherine

I know the death of the physical body isn't the end of individual awareness. The essence of the individual continues. From my experience, traditional notions of consciousness, dimensionality, and reality are far too limited. I experience reality energetically when I merge with a comatose, dying, or deceased person, or with the God source. When in that space, I engage in a type of communication that's so intimate, it seems to transcend the barriers of mind or space.

I now accept my gift as a blessing, both for me and the many people with whom I have worked. In my service to others, I, too, have grown myself. I know that death isn't the end of our individual expression and connections. Call it soul, spirit, or essence, the old adage still applies that wherever you go, you take yourself with you. Although we shed our bodies, our essential selves remain intact. Based on my experiences with people who have died, there is a freedom from our human attachment and fixation with dense form. The sense of separateness that so permeates how we live and experience people and things in this reality is transformed and transcended.

Our personal ideas and conceptualizations about life after death are wholly unique to us and based on many factors and experiences. When coupled with our liberation from particular states of consciousness and dimensionality, it seems our expectations form for us our unique and highly individual experiences of the afterlife. The language we use to describe heaven, the other side, another plane of reality, etc., is woefully inadequate, in my opinion because the vocabulary doesn't adequately designate the state or place. It's our beliefs and expectations that seem to be the powerful creative forming agents of the experience that awaits us at death. In other words, what you believe is often what you experience in the afterlife.

Though I have been privy to countless descriptions, discussions and revelations about the post-death experience, my understanding has been mainly forged through the God inspirations. There are no borders, no barriers, no divisions, no separations, and no linear or sequential frameworks in the afterlife. Instead, what awaits us is an expansive freedom, which is void of our mind's endless parceling out and dividing of our experiences and realities.

Entry into the hereafter isn't predicated on merit or belief. It doesn't require living or believing a certain way that guarantees passage into the afterlife. Every soul that loses its body has an experience in the afterlife. Release from this earthly existence gives way to welcoming the "All-in-Total" of unbounded love and connection that is infinite and expansive—a complete union and oneness that's transcendent in all ways. Although the deceased people's accounts and descriptions are fascinating, the consistent quality across all of them is this infinite love-based expression, experience and connection.

Our physical death expands us and provides us lots of new experiences. We can receive the keys to the kingdom. Finally, it's possible to merge or be one with the source of all love and creation. Our liberation from the body can also ripen us to receive a greater homecoming in spirit and soul. It's impossible to delineate all that awaits us, but it can include whatever you might conceive and believe for yourself.

Kevin died a physical death, but he neither disappeared nor ceased to be himself. His spirit and his essence continued. But because the deceased are gone from our sight, out of contact and communication, the silence can be deafening when we lose someone we love. We can take comfort in reminding ourselves their love and spirits are still with us.

After relaying hundreds of messages from deceased people and experiencing their essences, I know that they are only "gone" in a physical sense. I have tremendous empathy and compassion for those who are left grieving. The depth of their love and ongoing attachment is beautiful, profound, and steadfast. In many cases, to be with these loved ones is to witness a truly pure and, at a very elemental level, authentic and unalterable quality of love and connection.

Jocelyn exemplified grief, heartbreaking sadness and despair. Though she couldn't see it or feel it, she also reflected and exuded her pristine, exquisite, and pure love for Kevin. This love and attachment were now held in some paradoxical tension between a curse and a blessing. Those of us who have suffered and endured love and loss know this place of extreme vulnerability and implicit grace as a result of having loved so completely.

CHAPTER 77

AN INVALUABLE
GIFT OF PRESENCE

Catherine

ocelyn wanted deeply to reconnect with Kevin. I wanted to do any small thing I could to ease her loss and pain. The heart knows when it's ready to extend itself. Although I told Jocelyn that I would be happy to do another writing after Kevin's death, I didn't promise that he would connect with her. That really was a matter of God's grace and Kevin's soul's ability to engage.

I hadn't seen Jocelyn in almost six weeks. Both mentally and physically, she still looked exhausted and stressed. She seemed to simultaneously be in a state of silent dread and guarded expectation.

It's only natural to want to comfort the grieving, yet grief and loss are such intimate places of vulnerability and helplessness. We need to respect grief's rhythm, both in others and ourselves. It's a true gift to give space and honor to the griever's feelings, no matter how uncomfortable they may make us feel. It's an invaluable gift of presence to witness and embrace another's feelings without needing to immediately take action or eradicate them.

I've learned that just sitting in silence as a presence with the other is sometimes the most loving and healing thing we can do. Jocelyn and I sat at my dining room table. It was a sunny afternoon that didn't give any hint to the truth that there had been an absence of sunshine in Jocelyn's world since Kevin died.

As the writing began, Kevin and Jocelyn were once again united.

First
After-Death
Writing

October 15, 2013

CHAPTER 78

YOUR CENTER

Kevin, Jocelyn and Catherine

GOD: Welcome, Jocelyn. The tentacles are all moving. There is in this a fluidity that must move gently with all the tides and currents that are coming. You are invited to know this place of free movement. To be attached, yes, but able to be accommodating to whatever life's waters move and direct. Be this, be this, be this. This being has eight capable appendages that can hold and direct so many things, yet it is able to move and have no solid form. Not resorting to the strength of fists, but to direct inner strength and wisdom, to be responsive in a way that isn't in opposition to what the currents are bringing. You are in the deep waters, and holding your breath only works so long. Swimming and submerging your emotions and your daily presence, stop and pause to be yourself. This is necessary to know that you are more than these tentacles that service everyone and everything. These are attached to a center that contains not only the massive brain but a sensing, loving center that is not limited by all these boundaries of demands, problems, realities, and life factors. You are not such a developed being that you have forgotten your center.

You paddle, you dive, you go deeper, deeper, deeper, hoping and awaiting that surfacing into a familiar reality you once knew, where you might break the surface and this all be a dream. It is an awakened place that holds all the tentacles free from constant motion. But know it is okay to be held, to let yourself be held. Water is all about you in support, in that you can never actually sink. For you are your center. Your spirit, your heart IS …

I interrupted before God finished his introduction. This probably isn't the wisest thing to do when God is talking to you, but I really just wanted to talk to Kevin. This was the first writing since he died, and I didn't know whether I would actually get to talk to him.

I was a nervous wreck. After everything I had been through in the last three months, I desperately needed to talk to my husband. What if he was a no-show? In the last writing, we had talked about me trying to connect with him through Catherine after he died. Even though we had those unbelievable experiences of the writings when he was in UCLA and hospice, he was still alive then. I was worried that now he was gone, I would never get to talk to him again.

CHAPTER 79

I Had My Kevie Back!

JOCELYN: Kevin was always my center.

KEVIN: And you mine. Meet you in the middle, girlie. Meet you in the middle. Okay, I was holding myself back for that patient point of entry. It's God after all, but it is what it is. Take action and pray for forgiveness.

*I burst into tears as soon as Catherine said, "And you mine."
I had my Kevie back!*

KEVIN: Turns out God is the ultimate forgiver. Oh, here we are. My sweetheart, here we are. Chaperoned again, but I say thank you.

*I lack the patience gene. Kevin had it in spades. Good thing
I was forgiven for jumping in.*

JOCELYN: Are you okay?

KEVIN: Okay doesn't begin to capture it. This would be a 5 a.m. talk and we'd need to lock ourselves in. I'm in this place of unlimited "Oh, my gosh! Oh, my gosh!" I haven't got any words to describe it. I need you to help me. You'd be able to catch and convey it all. It's so much more than any of us have ever heard.

After his first surgery, Kevin would go to these early morning prayer meetings at 6:00 a.m. At the time, I had to drive him everywhere. He was only allowed to drive again after three months of being seizure-free. I hated those early morning prayer meetings. But it was important to him, so I took him. All these strange, overly religious, holier-than-thou people who wanted to put their hands on me and pray for me. So not my thing, especially before coffee.

Asking whether the deceased person is okay is the most common question I get. It's understandable, given that the afterlife is such a big black box. Kevin's response that he was surprised—that his expectations were exceeded, and that the experience defied explanation—wasn't uncommon from what other deceased people have reported.

CHAPTER 80

WHAT DID YOU SEE?

JOCELYN: Kevin, what did you see when you died?

KEVIN: It was a golden ray that just came all about the room and me. Just complete acceptance and love. I knew then that I was in this place I'd been trying to touch my entire life. It wasn't a visual as much as it was a complete experience from the inside out. It was wonder. It was love. It was knowing at the same instant how small I was and how infinitely large. It was like all the love I felt was magnified, and I was also a part of it myself. It was so surprising! It was—forgive me, Catherine, for being impolite, but this is an example that I think parallels well. It was like that place of orgasm or climax where you are so much not of the reality you know. You fall into some all-encompassing delight. So it was like this, only take orgasm and multiply it by infinity, and now you see why I was so full of wonder. It was pure wonder and awe.

JOCELYN: That's how you looked—blissed out.

I was lying next to Kevin in his bed when he took his last breath. Immediately after, he opened his eyes wide and let out what sounded like a surprised gasp. He hadn't opened his eyes in days and hadn't spoken for even longer. I had never seen that look on his face before. It was literally pure bliss. I turned to his best friend who was standing next to the bed and said, "Did you see that?" He had seen it too.

KEVIN: Good thing I didn't make another face you'd recognize. My apologies again, Catherine. But it is like that.

As you know, Kevin was always the spiritual one, whereas I lived in the physical world. Leave it to him to make an analogy I could totally relate to.

Kevin wasn't referencing a near-death experience, in which a person dies and comes back. What Jocelyn had witnessed was the moment of transition from life to death. This is the most sacred of moments. Kevin's surprised expression unequivocally convinced her that he was seeing and being received into an infinitely greater reality than we know.

JOCELYN: How come you don't talk to me by yourself?

KEVIN: I know that if our situations were reversed, you'd have figured this out. But I don't know how. So I outsourced, thankfully. I don't know how to talk to you directly. I'm with you. I try to let you know and I think, "Concentrate—feel me. I'm here." But there must be something that doesn't allow it.

JOCELYN: I do feel you all the time.

KEVIN: Yep, cause I'm there most of it. Especially when you collapse at night. I just see you breathe.

JOCELYN: Can you watch us all the time?

KEVIN: It's not like TV. There are privacies that are in place. Sort of a parental control by God maybe. Inopportune times, no. For you, since we shared all facets of our lives, there appear not to be the same restrictions. So for example, I can be with our kids but I am not watching their private moments. Their moments of deep emotion, yes. But then it's not a seeing, it's a feeling.

JOCELYN: The kids say they feel you all the time.

KEVIN: Because they need to know I'm not gone. They have been hit hard.

JOCELYN: You're right.

KEVIN: It has taken the very foundation out from under them.

JOCELYN: True.

KEVIN: They will, in time, be better. But it's as if the ground they knew isn't the ground anymore. We didn't know, you and me, what we have given the kids. We thought maybe we bungled it at times, but to our credit we are solid footing to them. I'm impressed with us. But now it's moving under them. You always were the concrete one—and me, well, the mop-up guy.

JOCELYN: That's not true.

KEVIN: It is true. You were the solid "here we are" girl. I was, "Well, yes and maybe. Maybe we can soften it up here and there." I didn't realize how we complemented each other even in our parenting. But from this vantage point, which is beyond any expansiveness I'd have thought possible before arriving, I see it all from another position.

CHAPTER 81

I'm Worried

JOCELYN: What about Chris? He's a train wreck right now.

Chris' addiction was worse than ever at this point.

KEVIN: He is and has been. I'm worried. I'm so sorry for all you are left to contend with. This is the place that makes me sigh the loudest.

JOCELYN: Do you know what he's been up to?

KEVIN: He's using heavily. He talks a good game, and yet he's so far out there he scares himself. Then he pays lip service to try to exorcise his demons, but it's like all the other times—hollow. He's out of control. I'm not angry. I'm exasperated that I'm not there at least for us to be co-sanity monitors.

JOCELYN: You can't influence this at all with him?

KEVIN: If I could, I would have on day one.

JOCELYN: Will can't stand him because he scares him.

KEVIN: His heart has every right to these emotions. He is such a love bucket. This is not right, and I'm so sorry you are enduring all this. At least when I was there—as helpless as the rest of us,

I grant you that—but at least Will didn't feel defenseless. He now feels like he has to protect you. It's too much for him, and it's not how he should be spending his youth. And I don't think that Chris' problems should psychologically stunt Will, but I fear they will.

Kevin and I always called Will "Love Bucket." In all the writings I've had, Kevin always uses the same terms of endearment he used in life that were personal to us.

JOCELYN: Will resents me for not protecting him.

KEVIN: It's not resentment, its verbalized helplessness.

Not only was I dealing with Kevin's death, but I was also trying to help Chris, while at the same time protecting Will from the fallout from Chris' addiction. It was an impossible situation and I felt like road kill. Especially with Kevin gone, I so wanted for Will to have a loving and healthy relationship with his brother, which was impossible at the time.

JOCELYN: How is Will aside from this?

KEVIN: A mess. He internalizes so much. He's like you in this. You hold yourself together by the sheer force of will, but the insides are a big bounce house and no one is having any fun.

JOCELYN: I made him go back to school. I thought you would want me to do that.

KEVIN: It was the best decision. At least eight hours a day he knows what to expect. No trauma, no drama. I did want you to send him back to school and I'm glad you did. It's even good for his mind to be occupied.

CHAPTER 82

FIJI

JOCELYN: The kids and I are going to take your ashes to Fiji.

KEVIN: I know. I wish I was there board-side.

> *Kevin had always wanted to surf in Fiji. I decided to take his ashes to the surf spot where he always wanted to go and put them in the surf. When he was alive, he had a surf trip planned to Fiji with the Surfing Lawyers of California, a group of lawyer surfers who take surf trips together and do continuing education presentations at night so the trip is a write-off.*
>
> *A few weeks before the planned Fiji trip, there was a death in my family and so Kevin cancelled. I still wanted him to go, but he didn't want to leave me. It was so typical of him, always putting me first. I'd always felt bad that he didn't go on that trip because it had been his surfing fantasy for as long as I knew him. Since Kevin didn't have that experience when he was alive, I wanted to take his ashes to Fiji so he could at least have it in some way.*

JOCELYN: I just miss you so much.

KEVIN: Oh, and I you. But we are at 99.99% now. You are my light, my love, my everything. I want you to know I am infinitely blessed and loved. Heaven on earth, that's what you are. I'm so glad you are no longer on Kevie Death Watch—how droll! Thank you for not taking me home. I had no idea it was going to be that quick. It was better at hospice.

> *While Kevin often called me Joc, more often than not he referred to me using some term of endearment like love, sweetie, or doll. He always told me he loved me, adored me, treasured me. It isn't just something he started doing in these writings.*
>
> *Catherine had never seen us interact with each other and didn't know that we always referred to each other in these sappy terms of endearment. After she started these writings, she asked me whether that was a new thing. Catherine found it hard to believe that we referred to each other so lovingly after being together over 25 years. I believe her comment was, "Who does that?"*
>
> *I figured Kevin's 99.99% comment was a reference to what he said in his last UCLA writing—that he knew me better when he was almost dead than when he was alive because now, we were "heart-to-heart." During that UCLA writing, Kevin joked that he was approaching 90%, so his 99.99% reference had to be related to that concept.*

JOCELYN: I had no idea either [*referring to the fact he would die that quickly*].

KEVIN: You were making in-home rehab plans. I'm so grateful to Catherine for coming down there and changing that plan, and for coming to help our family.

JOCELYN: Is there anything you want me to do or think I should be doing?

KEVIN: I think you should really go into that well that you fear.

JOCELYN: What well?

KEVIN: The one where you feel how shitty this is, how you are breaking within. You'll come out.

JOCELYN: I actually feel I'm handling things pretty well.

KEVIN: You always do and have. It doesn't mean there isn't an enough-is-enough point. I always could call you on your mighty-woman-on-steroids tendency. All I'm saying is when you start to lose it, let yourself. Okay? Don't judge yourself or suck it up. You have swallowed enough tears that another person would have drowned by now. I love you—utterly, completely, to the universe, and to all the places in between. I miss your smell, your touch, your breath on my neck. I miss it all. But we're at 99.99%. That physical knowing and touching is minor in comparison to this.

> *It seemed Kevin and God were tag teaming to encourage Jocelyn to feel all her feelings. Why do we humans tend to batten down the hatches by erecting walls and barriers to contain our emotions, thinking it's healthy and will give us more strength and power?*

CHAPTER 83

AM I GOING TO
SEE YOU AGAIN?

JOCELYN: Am I going to see you again?

This is the one question I really wanted answered the most yet was afraid to ask. What if the answer was no? After Kevin died, that was the one thing I wanted to believe more than anything, that we would be together again. I hoped it was true, but I didn't really believe it. I wasn't religious and didn't have faith in God or even really believe God existed. If there was a God, I had been cursing him daily for taking Kevin from me. I was irrationally worried that I had pissed off a God I wasn't even sure existed, and my punishment would be that I wouldn't get to see Kevin again.

KEVIN: Yes! I don't mean as an apparition. I mean that God and I have had a long, long talk. It was beautiful. Yes, we are to be reunited. And yes, it will be as if not one second has passed. I know we will be together, and then nothing can separate us. Jesus said that "love knows no divisions. This is a veil, but love knows no divisions." And then he smiled and embraced me. Can you imagine—Jesus is a great hugger? Who would have thought it? I mean yes, I believed in Jesus. But it is possible to meet Jesus, talk to him, and get a hug from him!

> *When Kevin said I would be with him again, the relief was overwhelming. I knew that if I was going to get to be with him again, I could live through anything until I arrived there—especially if it was going to feel like not one second had passed. I think about that a lot now, when the days seem long and I feel frazzled and overwhelmed trying to handle everything on my own.*

JOCELYN: I bet that made you really happy.

KEVIN: Happy, yes! But the whole thing was so affirming on all levels. A direct experience of spirit. This place of God's embrace is not like anything I've ever read or studied.

> *Kevin's spirituality was not in the lip-service kind of way, like when people say they are spiritual to make you think they don't really care about materialistic things, but you know they'd choose a Ferrari over spirituality any day. Kevin really was spiritual in the truest sense of the word. It permeated everything he did. He was always reading a spiritual book, going to seminars, studying with friends, and he took his Bible with him every day when he left the house. I always knew what his schedule was, and I would often say to him when he had a full day, "Why are you bringing your Bible? You won't have any time to read it today." He would reply, "I just like to have it with me."*

> In life and the afterlife, our preset expectations and the boundaries of our beliefs can color and mandate what we allow ourselves to experience. Kevin was a Christian, so Jesus being part of his welcoming committee wasn't surprising. But a loved one hugged

by Jesus was new to me. What a reception! All the post-death experiences in the writings are unique to the individual, though there are commonalities.

The mainstream idea of death as a car wash the soul goes into and comes out of spic and span represents an oversimplification. Sometimes folks who don't have spiritual or religious foundations or alignments seem more timid and uncertain about this loving, cosmic embrace. Often they can benefit from the extra encourage-ment to jump fully into this new, freeing, universal, soul and love experience.

Kevin didn't need this counsel. To the contrary, it sounded like he was joyfully welcomed to the home he had always expected. His pre-death clarity, conviction, and embodied faith seemed to serve him in this wondrous expansion beyond the physical realm. That said, he did share that it exceeded his expectations. Would we expect any less than this for the all-loving, all-encompassing divine reception that awaits each of us upon our death?

CHAPTER 84

GO WITH THE REASONABLE

JOCELYN: I'm having a life celebration for you.

I hate memorial services. Who doesn't? I didn't want to have anything like that for Kevin. But many people asked me about it, so I decided I owed it to everyone who loved Kevin to celebrate his life. We had talked about it when he was alive. He knew I hated those things and told me he just wanted me to do what I wanted to do, and not do anything I didn't want to do out of pressure or a sense of obligation.

KEVIN: Yes, but don't spend a ton of money, okay? If I can't drink the wine, go with the reasonable. Video it—spend the extra there so that the kids and my grandchildren might have it. You know, my whole life I tried to be helpful, to make a difference. I think I did in small ways.

Even though Kevin loved a good bottle of red wine, he would never buy himself the expensive stuff. I wanted him to have the good stuff, especially after he was initially diagnosed. I always bought expensive bottles of wine and took the tag off the bottle, then lied to him about what it cost. He always asked me whether it was an expensive bottle and I would say, "No, it was reasonable." I realized he knew I was lying, but I didn't care. I didn't want him drinking crappy wine when he only had a few wine drinking years left.

I'm so glad I took his advice and had his life celebration videotaped. I've watched it many times. It's affirming to see so many people share their wonderful memories of Kevin. I heard stories about him I had never heard before, including ways he touched the lives of people I never knew. He really was a humble man and never tooted his own horn, even though he easily could have. People who came and spoke about him didn't really talk about Kevin's many accomplishments, but rather what it meant to them to have had him in their lives. I wasn't the only person who loved him and felt the loss when he died. I'm really glad I sucked it up and had the celebration, even though it was the last thing I wanted to do so soon after he died.

JOCELYN: Did you read the letter I wrote that first night, the one I used for the obituary?

KEVIN: I loved it! But I was right next to you as you wrote it. Your words circled around my spirit like a breeze of such love. Your heart, the feelings that poured forth from there, they are better than any warm waters. They love me. They make me a brighter being. You have always made me a better person. You have always called me to my greatness because you have always been like a homing beacon, calling me, guiding me, loving me. If I could draw a picture of it—and I can't, as you know—it would look more like stick art. You are my lighthouse.

We have been through a lifetime of experiences and have loved each other in all weathers. You have been that loving light that has always been there for me, and I for you. Though you can't see me, feel my light. Feel my love guiding, helping in all ways. I can help navigate. But the light, it's blinding. There wasn't a tunnel or any of that stuff. Just that brilliant, bathing, loving light, and I was held in your loving light when it appeared. You, my wife, my soul partner, we will never be parted because I realized that loving you and being loved by you was and is holy. I am Wholly Spirit because you helped me be the soul I am. I'm so grateful, my heart is bursting.

Go and eat. I wish I could join you—it would be my pleasure. I love you.

GOD: Go with God.

> Kevin's presence and strength couldn't have come at a more needed moment. During the writing, Jocelyn received a call that all hell had broken out at home. In Jocelyn's ongoing nightmare of loss, pain, and anguish, Kevin had found a way to thank, love, and help support her.

CHAPTER 85

WITH ME

Jocelyn

I got my answer—our relationship didn't die with Kevin. While he wasn't here with me physically, he wasn't gone. I had felt him next to me when I wrote that letter to the cosmos. To hear him say that in the writing made me realize that all the times since then when I felt him with me, he really was with me. What I wrote about him in that letter was nothing compared to what he was saying to me now and had been saying through all the writings.

He made me a better person, not the other way around. I was a brighter being because of him, not the other way around. But it was so typical of Kevin to make it about me and not about himself. To now really know that he was with me in all ways, even though I couldn't see him, made me feel that he wasn't really gone. Kevin may not be here with me in the physical sense, but he is with me in all other ways. I never wanted to be apart from him, and now I knew we weren't. I was beyond grateful—to him for everything he was and everything he is, and to Catherine for having this gift that let us still be together.

Catherine and I had planned on going out to lunch after this writing, which Kevin obviously knew from his "go eat, I wish I could join you" comment. It would be the first time we ever did something social together unrelated to these writings and the start of what would become a great friendship. You would think having a friend who could communicate with God and dead people would be kind of weird, but it's not. Her gift isn't the basis of our friendship. Laughter is.

We have so much fun when we are hanging out together. We both have the same irreverent sense of humor, which is kind of funny because "reverent" is what most people would imagine someone like Catherine to be. We both always say what's on our mind without thinking much about it first, or not at all. We have similar intellects and both of us have a bit of a potty mouth. We really are very much alike except, of course, that she can communicate with God and dead people, and I can't. I tell myself I have other skill sets, but it's hard to top hers.

CHAPTER 86

INNER WISDOM

Catherine

In her eagerness to reconnect with Kevin, Jocelyn interrupted God's introduction to the writing. I don't think she heard a word of it. We can all relate to the tentacles image—needing to manage or control everything in our life and being pulled in several directions at once. Attempting to grasp, understand, and respond to all the people, things, and situations in our life (sometimes in vain) can leave us feeling spread too thin and exhausted. In our fast-paced society, we seem to be drowning in our to-do lists and decisions that must be made. I would love to have the eight appendages God talked about to handle life's complex and often competing demands.

Jocelyn had been cast adrift in deep, uncharted waters without her steadfast life mate Kevin. Losing him had unmoored her from the reality she had known her whole adult life. God echoed the need to be gentle with herself. God seemed to be urging her to be flexible, and move unconstrained and boldly forward, even during this painful time. It's sage advice to try to be flexible in how we deal with problems, situations, and people in times of uncertainty and loss. Erecting more barriers to our own self-embrace, self-honoring, and acceptance of our feelings only serves to exacerbate our pain and anger. The tenor of all our attempts to deny feelings can leave us overwhelmed. Creating a pause or quiet moment of peace in the onslaught of thoughts and emotions can enable us to be softer, clearer, and more responsive.

We can overcome our tendencies to become more rigid and a hostage to our pain and anger. By not turning to fist-fighting what is, we allow space for our own inner wisdom and strength to emerge and lift us. This advice applies to the mundane challenges of daily existence as well as to major life events. We can unconsciously slip into autopilot and keep on going, minimizing and unrelentingly pushing ourselves.

Jocelyn was cautioned that this was a kind of breath-holding submergence and suspension of living, all of which were unsustainable. Eventually her anger and pain would outmatch her. She was directed to breathe life back into herself by connecting with her inner source, heart, and spirit. Our heart, our center and spirit, ultimately are our truest sources of wisdom, guidance, and strength.

Jocelyn was being reminded of how we can become so focused on others that we fail to care for ourselves. Sometimes we can become an afterthought, or no thought, in the equation of our lives. The lack of balance and ignoring our own needs can leave us feeling depleted, ineffective and ultimately resentful. Many of us imagine that if we grit or power our way through, using all our tentacles to manage, master, or override reality, maybe we can out-swim the undertow of life's difficulties or unbearable situations. We believe that a "mind over matter" mentality, by which we mean our will, can counteract being overloaded and overwhelmed. When we rely on our brain and strategies to stay afloat in our own sea of powerlessness, this mode can become so habitual that we may forget our heart altogether.

"Water is all about you in support, in that you can never actually sink. For you are your center. Your spirit, your heart IS …"

Our heart and center are our ever-present power sources. They are unsinkable life and love preservers. It isn't through our mind alone that we survive, but through our heart and center that we thrive and grow. Our center is infinitely one with our spirit or soul, which buoys us in the deepest of life's waters. Power, love, and strength are within us. We can never drown by anchoring ourselves in love, spirit, and connection. It's that inner relationship within us that allows us to enhance, expand, grow, and transform.

CHAPTER 87

A FOOT IN BOTH REALMS

Catherine

After the writing session with Kevin, Jocelyn was jubilant. Words don't convey what it's like for me to dip into these kinds of energy fields. I hold a foot in both realms, but my heart is the sensor and conductor of the energy that connects them. Perhaps this is heart-to-heart communication. It's as if I can sense and receive the other's essential essence and energy beyond their personality in the traditional sense. As I touched on earlier, their messages come not as words but something much more intimate and expansive, almost like a primordial essence. It's their energy, their essential soul if you will, that communicates.

I use the word "communicate" but it's only shorthand for sensing the divine, calibrating and merging with the energy, feelings, and oneness experience. Much like when we dialogue with others in this reality, we sense, interpret, and attach meaning beyond their mere words. My gift allows me to translate and share this energy with loved ones.

Unlike overhearing a couple whisper sweet nothings to each other, when Kevin expresses the depth of his love for Jocelyn, there is also a sound, a texture, a depth, and an energetic beauty. His love, the energetics of it, has a certain quality to it that is so much more than just loving expressions or compliments. It's like the experience of seeing the most beautiful scene in nature, wrapped in the smile of a baby, combined with the iridescent feathers of a hummingbird, and joined with the tickle of a belly laugh. It's fluid love, not able to be frozen into any form.

Although formless like that of other deceased people, Kevin's love felt as real as my own experiences of earthly human love. It's as if I am a fountain, feeling these very fluid and powerful energies and emotions. The magnitude of these emotions, thoughts, and memories all wrap together as one.

This is only one aspect of the many personal blessings of my gift. Each time I do a session, I am widened, transformed and expanded. My own capacity to love, experience, and embody this divine energy is magnified. By remaining free of any agenda and not directing or being attached to particular outcomes, my ability to transmit the energy and intentions with the same level of authenticity and purity is further honed. Despite all these direct experiences of the divine and other spirits, I remain humbled.

If the world could experience one thimbleful of the God energy, it would change in a nanosecond. Tragically, we humans are caught in our own constructions of separation, limitation, and barriers. Unknowingly, we have become accustomed to our exclusionary reliance on a fearful and mind-based sense of reality, and we are not even aware of it. While it doesn't fully serve us, it's the limited way in which humanity has approached the nature of reality for millennia. In my work over these many years, God has offered what I call the Loveality® teachings as an alternative love-based approach to welcome and experience reality. Whereas the mind prejudges, protects, polarizes, and condemns, Loveality® welcomes authentic, loving, and divine connection. This kind of love and connection lets us embrace our lives and experiences with radical and unbounded gratitude.

The truth is that love is in every atom, expression, creation, and essence. We are constantly in a state of becoming. What a spectacular way of being emerges once we realize we can set down our mental burdens and dispense with fear, division, lack, and limitations. When we inhabit reality and our lives with infinite love, what an invitation for transformation and transcendence through genuine heart-and-soul-filling experiences.

CHAPTER 88

I FELT KEVIN'S ENERGY

Catherine

Over the years I've noticed that water in various forms seems to be a conductor or amplifier of my receptivity to God and spirit energy. The water amplifying connection can result from being near a large body of water, a hot tub or pool, or in the shower. I try to start every day with prayer, usually in the shower. My prayer always begins like this:

> Hello God. I invite the Holy Spirit into my heart and soul. I thank you for giving me this day to live and love and learn. I ask that today your will be done. I ask for the wisdom to discern your will for me in my life, and the courage to do the things I feel you are calling me to do.

After this beginning, I pray for others, situations, the world, and myself. I invite a connection with God. For me it's through the Holy Spirit, although I respect that the names, expressions, and conceptualizations of this divine energy and presence differ for each of us. In my welcoming, I affirm my state of gratitude, openness, and willingness to be directed by the divine and be of service to others. I acknowledge that I don't always know what's in my own best interest or good.

Meditation, prayer, and my work are the primary conduits I use to connect with divine energy. Each of us has our own particular path that speaks to us. I believe the divine doesn't play favorites but gives us unlimited opportunities to express, connect, and expand our spiritual selves. None of us can judge the value of spiritual connection for another. Yet we see the inherent dangers when religion or spirituality is used to dominate, oppress or control people.

Regardless of our preferred way to connect, most of us long for the experience of this kind of prized, profound, and personal soul connection. It doesn't matter the form our spirituality takes, formal or informal. Just being in nature, we are served by fostering our own personal connection with our soul. It may not always be simple or easy. It's invaluable for me to reaffirm this connection daily, along with my desire to serve and be in harmony with the deeper rhythm of my soul.

The day after Jocelyn's first writing following Kevin's death, I felt Kevin's energy as I was praying in the shower. Although I had become accustomed to his gentleness, the nonintrusive and respectful manner in which he signals and connects with me is remarkable. My sense of him is consistent with the man his friends and family describe. His energy was quiet, with the lightest impression and touch. Although apologetic, he was emphatic about wanting me to write again. Once I was dressed, I got my pen and paper, then began to write.

CHAPTER 89

NOT A HAPPY BIRTHDAY

Jocelyn

My birthday is on October 16. I had just had a writing with Catherine the day before. I hadn't told her that my birthday was coming up. There wasn't anything to celebrate. I felt guilty even thinking about my birthday when Kevin would never have another one. Kevin's birthday was on September 28, just a few weeks before mine. Had he lived just 21 days longer, he would have been 60 when he died.

When I awakened on my birthday, all I felt was despair. Kevin loved birthdays and holidays, whereas I thought they were a hassle. Before my birthday or a holiday, he always took the kids out to buy me clothes that usually didn't fit me and I'd have to return. He always made such a big deal out of my birthday, telling me that it was the best holiday ever because it was the day I was born. Who wouldn't love someone to think this about them?

On every birthday from the time we were first together, the first thing he said when he woke up in the morning was "Happy Birthday, Joc," which would be followed by hugs and kisses, and of course the daily flower on my pillow. When the kids were young, he made them breakfast and got them ready for the day. He almost always took my birthday off work, just to spend the entire day with me. We would go out for breakfast and read the *Los Angeles Times* cover to cover, then maybe take a walk on the beach. Even though I always told him not to do anything special and not to buy me any gifts, he always ignored me and went all out.

So when I woke up on my 51st birthday, alone in our Cal King bed, it wasn't a happy birthday at all.

There was no way I was going into work that day. I just wasn't feeling it. After I took our son to school, I went to the local grocery store to buy mimosa fixings and load up on carbs. I was going to have a pity party instead of a birthday party. I was feeling sorry for myself, mad at the universe, and more alone than I'd ever felt in my life.

While I was waiting in line at the grocery store, my cell phone rang. It was Catherine. She asked me if it was my birthday. I asked her how she could possibly know. I hadn't told her my birthday was coming up, so there was no way she could have known. I later asked my sister whether she had told Catherine it was my birthday, and she hadn't.

Catherine said she had a birthday present for me. If I was free, I could drive by her house and pick it up. So after I left the grocery store with champagne, orange juice, and enough Danish pastries to give myself a heart attack, I drove to her house, wondering what kind of present she had for me. Explaining that Kevin had wanted to wish me a happy birthday, she handed me some papers she had stapled together.

I took the papers, drove out of her driveway, and parked on the street. I couldn't wait to see what was written. I had just talked to Kevin the day before and he hadn't mentioned my upcoming birthday. I didn't know and hadn't even considered that when someone dies, they can still keep track of dates here on earth.

As you know, all of Catherine's writings start with a God introduction. I have always just glossed over those, because all I ever wanted was to talk to Kevin. Since this was an unsolicited writing, there were both a lengthy God introduction and a birthday message from Kevin.

Birthday Writing

October 16, 2013

CHAPTER 90

NEW LIFE

Kevin and Catherine

GOD: Welcome, Jocelyn.

The sentence is a statement. It has a complete expression of a thought, concept, or example. But a sentence, though it possesses a period at its ending, does not mean there aren't more sharings, stories, connections, and pairings to continue. For a period appears to mark an ending, a thing that says, "Now you are here in the conceptualization, but a new sentence follows." It does not lead, it continues. So the "hows" and "whats" that the mind requests and even demands punctuation for aren't the language of the heart and soul. For the mind says, "I must see it to experience it. I must collapse my experiences into segmented and discriminate realities for the purpose of my linear nature." The heart and soul hold no such artificial or contrived boundaries. Though it appears to the physical eye that something has ended, to the heart and soul it isn't so. For love is unending and eternal, as is soul—connection vowed and sealed so deep within that it does not end with a physical passage or ending. No, the love in its fluid nature pours itself forth without the need for a vessel or a bodily cup to contain or express it. For love is greater than all these languages that the mind engages.

This introduction was so apropos. I think it was referring to our life as a statement. If so, then our life doesn't end with death. Death isn't a period or an ending. Contrary to the mind's linear nature about divisions and endings, our heart and soul are all about love and soul eternal.

GOD: Love is unlimited. It is birthed within and it has no end. It is eternal, as you are. Allow the warmth of love, that light between you and the beloved, to cradle you in arms that now seem formless but are more expansive and stronger than they have ever been.

That chorus of Happy Birthday that to the mind rings hollow, soundless, and empty. Happy is a fragment, a filament of light in memory that is dancing on the shadow of loss and missing. But warm yourself to that light of love, that though the period has appeared in the physical, it still burns bright. Not an ember, but a brilliant lighthouse saying, "In this place of our deep love and joining, I am guiding, loving, ever present, steering you to me by the light of this love we share." This love that two know can be as the divine extension of self, of soul, of connection, of union, knows not the silence nor the distance.

Love's presence as light, warmth, and strength permeated the message. The enduring connection between Jocelyn and Kevin could never be extinguished. More astoundingly, their connection was expanded and strengthened after Kevin's death.

GOD: It is the heart that speaks to the beloved. It is the heart that crosses a seeming divide that separates the realities of life and "New Life." It is not to an afterlife that God sends your beloved. This is to place the emphasis on "after" life, as if life was the most celebrated and worthy. No, it is New Life. Yes, and in New Life the beloved toasts and is animated with grace and gratefulness. For all is real, the expressions and forms no longer held in the linear bounded reality.

New Life celebrates all. New Life knows that blood is only necessary in body, that breath is only necessary in body. But love—love stands as the very essence of all creation in all realms, life or New Life. Life is love, and love is life—and this cannot be severed, no matter.

The idea of New Life rather than an "afterlife" is profoundly liberating. New Life transcends the concept of something lost or ended. It also dispenses with our identification with the body as the only source of valuable expression and incarnation. The heart, the ever-present eternal essence, was being juxtaposed with the mind's attachments to linear holdings and divisions. In New Life our essence and expression are freed from the linear realities. Love is the eternal thread that is unbreakable regardless.

GOD: On this celebration, which is a marker, a year of passage from one year of life to the new year of life—a celebration without the physical embodiment of the beloved—know that love continues. It isn't a period. It isn't an ending. It is like a birth that has come to form and vitality, so strong, so vibrant, so eternal. A physical separation even in this most extreme form, death cannot diminish the real, potent, omnipresent, all-encompassing heart and soul in union with heart and soul in the divine covenant of marriage. It should not be till death do us part, because death has no say in the life and the New Life, for life is love eternal.

Your beloved raises the glass to drink from this eternal cup of love and union. Happy birthday! Your beloved awaits you in New Life, when your day comes, to drink in one reality. Though you do not see and are not holding each other, do not believe the shadows. No, turn to that lighthouse of love emanating within you, within the beloved, and eternally connected. Let this be your candle. Love—a period possesses no power over it. It is a union that says this story is without end. Be held in the warmth of the beloved, who raises a glass and praises your love—you in all your phases, celebrations, challenges, and expressions. Your beloved, who so loves and cherishes you, as you do him.

Happy birthday, not a refrain by tarrying in the death, but being warmed and illuminated by the radiant blaze of love between you, that nothing has any power to separate. What the mind can't see, the heart knows to be real. A toast to all the years of love together in full expression. A celebration of a life not ended, but turned into New Life. Alive, vibrant, zestful, but encompassed and amplified and expanded in the divine union with you and the beloved.

This is God's way. Not the vocabulary of endings, not the punctuation of loss and longing, not the punishment or forgetting, but the way of divine union. Your innate capacity is to join in divine love, which a physical body has no power to dictate over. Divine love, birthed between you and the beloved, brings heaven and form to earth in full expression. Toast to you for the birth and life you are expressing in all the infinite ways you subscribe in your free will and creativity to live it! Toast to you for the New Life of your beloved, which has only you in soul and heart still!

Happy birthday, for this year you may seem to be in shadow and are the experience of loss that is very real. Look to that lighthouse of love and see it is the beloved who stands beholding the light of your spirit, which even grief cannot eclipse. In the arms of your beloved and God you are held and cherished. A glass is raised in your honor to acknowledge the steadfast love you so wrapped, and cared, and shared, and experienced, and delighted in—and in all ways nourished, tended, nurtured, and beheld.

So no candles on the cake perhaps, or songs of celebration in your reality, but behold the light of the beloved on this and all days, celebrating you as you celebrate and cherish him.

Love has no period. Union has no end. Life to New Life, you and the beloved, eternally connected in heart and soul. This is the gift that has no end!

Go with God.

Jocelyn was being acknowledged and toasted. She was being celebrated for the depths of the love that dwelled inside her and that was her lighthouse. By living and loving their lives together, Jocelyn and Kevin had built this lighthouse of love. Their lighthouse was available to guide and illuminate Jocelyn. She was infinitely loved and cherished, not just by Kevin but also by God. The same is true for each of us. Infinite love embraces and connects us.

"Love has no period." Why then do we insist that death is the final ending? Why do we exclusively give all the power and emphasis to life in this earthly realm, but then fail to fully receive it as a gift? Why do so many of us question the way we live and love only when there's a threat that our life or love will be taken away or ended?

New Life doesn't just sit on the other side of death. Each day, each moment we live, each of us can lay claim to New Life. We don't have to wait for an afterlife to fully be ourselves—to experience and be this infinite love and connection. We can own it fully right now. At any time, we can open, engage, and embody ourselves and our own lives more freely and unconstrainedly, revealing and being our love and spirit-filled essence.

The next part of the writing is from Kevin.

CHAPTER 91

HAPPY BIRTHDAY

KEVIN: I was going to rent a top-down coupe and surprise you. I had volleyed lots of ideas around, never having a thought I wouldn't be there with you. And so, instead of what I so wanted to share with you, I've only made it a harder day.

I pulled through a bit for the anniversary. But this seems to be the most efficient way—the only one really, thanks to Catherine, for me to say Happy Birthday. You would have been showered with my love and attention from sunup to sundown, and even a little post sundown celebration as well.

You know, I wish I knew a way to surprise you. I'm a fledgling, a newbie, but I shall try—so keep your eyes open. My mastery or failure are not telltale signs of my devoted and universal love and treasuring of you—my heart, my gal, my tough as nails, heart of passion, and love deeper than any well known to any man.

So I'm not going to tell you to be happy, because you aren't going to listen. And what's to be happy about? I'd have much rather surprised you. But I will ask that you tolerate attention. That you let the kids see that normal is going to dinner—and yes, sticking a candle in a darn piece of cake. All these things, though half-hearted, are full-hearted, and I'll be there with all my lovies.

I love you! I will try for a surprise, but I'm new, so don't be upset if it's a little delayed. Who knows? You never knew what to expect. I'm the only one who got really good at surprising you. Let's see what this new skill set gets us.

I love you! Be on the lookout, Birthday Baby.

GOD: Go with God.

CHAPTER 92

LOOK, IT'S KEVIN

Jocelyn

When I finished reading the writings while stopped on the street outside Catherine's driveway, I didn't go home and drown my sorrows in mimosas and cheese Danishes. Instead, I drove to San Ysidro Ranch, where Kevin and I were married in the garden. I just walked around, soaking him in, because I knew he was there with me.

That evening I took the kids out to dinner, like we always did on a birthday. I let them sing Happy Birthday when the waiter brought dessert with a birthday candle in it. It wasn't a happy birthday, but Kevin was right. I needed to do it for the kids. Because he said he'd be right there with us, I also wanted to do it so that he could still celebrate too.

After my birthday, I kept my eyes peeled, waiting for whatever surprise he was going to attempt to give me. A few days later, I was sitting in the living room with our kids. Our dogs, a German Shepherd and a Doberman, were in the backyard and started barking furiously at something. I looked through the window out into the backyard. There was a squirrel on the fence staring straight at me. The dogs were jumping on the fence, trying to get at the squirrel. The fence was shaking from them lunging so hard against it. But the squirrel just sat on the top, unmoving, staring straight at me.

I told the kids to look at the squirrel on the fence, because I was sure it was a sign from Kevin. I even told them, "Look, it's Kevin!" For some odd reason, when Kevin and I talked about each other to the kids, we referred to each other by our first names, and not as mom and dad. We all watched the squirrel for what seemed like a long time, just looking at us while the dogs barked at it furiously. I'd never, in the 15 years I'd lived in that house or since that day, seen a squirrel on the fence or in the yard. I knew it was Kevin.

Kevin had a thing for squirrels. On our trips to Lake Arrowhead or Bass Lake, or anywhere in the mountains where there were squirrels, he bought unshelled peanuts for them. He lined them up on the deck or fence railing so the squirrels could come and eat them. He used to look out of the window and watch them grab a nut, crack it open, and eat it. Before going to bed, he once again lined the railing with nuts. He was always laughing in the morning when all that was left were the peanut shells on the deck.

We went to Lake Arrowhead relatively frequently. In fact, the last family trip we ever took was there for my son's thirteenth birthday, two weeks before Kevin's second surgery. On the drive there, even though it was on a mountain road where we could plummet to our deaths if the car went over the edge, Kevin often took his eyes off the road, pointed, and said, "Squirrel!" I can't tell you how many times I had to tell him to just please keep his eyes on the road, as a squirrel sighting wasn't worth our untimely deaths.

So when I saw the squirrel on the fence, where I had never seen one before, and the squirrel just stayed there totally still while the dogs were frantically trying to get it, I knew it was Kevin. It had to be, I had no doubt. I had gotten my birthday surprise in a form that was personal to me. He knew I would recognize this as a sign from him. In a later writing, he said that yes, the squirrel was a sign from him.

CHAPTER 93

DIVINE SYNCHRONICITIES

Catherine

A few days after the special delivery of her birthday writing, Jocelyn shared the peculiar squirrel experience she believed was Kevin fulfilling his promise to surprise her. I told her that this wasn't an uncommon experience, and that in the writings deceased people sometimes point out particular events they have purposely used to connect with their loved ones.

It doesn't have to be like Hollywood versions of ghosts or apparitions, but spirits' energies can attach to different things and temporarily become one with those things. I clarified that, unlike popularized stories or our fears, a spiritual embodiment of this type shouldn't be viewed as malevolent or a kind of possession. God has explained in other writings that the soul still likes to have sensory experiences, so sometimes the soul will briefly merge with another energy to have an experience. The attached energy doesn't override or take over the other's mind, soul, or body. It wasn't that Kevin was transformed into a squirrel, but rather he could attach himself to living things or even objects.

These experiences are powerful and can bring us out of our routinized ways of perceiving and making sense of reality. There's nothing like a direct experience to expand us beyond our current thought boundaries and limitations. These seemingly impossible experiences, some tiny and some dramatic, all signify that spirit and connection are always available to each of us.

There is wisdom in our hearts that whispers to us, if we listen. It can be a memory, a longing, a nudge, a novel thought, or an experience that our rational mind can't explain. Unusual experiences like these can also be a kind of heart-to-heart communication.

These are common to all of us. Sometimes we listen, whereas other times we dismiss them and may possibly miss the opportunity to listen and connect more deeply with ourselves. Many of us imagine we must travel somewhere else to learn or grow in our capacity to think and experience a larger reality. For Jocelyn, the opportunity to evolve her concept of reality and connection occurred right in her own backyard.

We are "sense-making machines" who choose what we allow to impact and shape our beliefs. Jocelyn was looking to me to help provide a template to understand these extraordinary experiences and had questions about this previously unknowable or ungraspable reality. Indeed, I have facilitated, experienced, or heard about hundreds of these inexplicable stories. My conclusion is simple—they are real and all of us have them.

Over the years, I've come to believe our commonly held conceptualizations of reality aren't always true. They only represent a fraction of the infinite love and creation of the whole that we are all joyously a part of. There is a greater and more expansive whole that doesn't rely on the mind's arbitrary designations, separations, or fear-based machinations. We are all Wholly Spirit and part of a Wholly All-In-Total from which we can never be separated. Our physical body reaches its expiration date, but our spirit is eternal. The invisible threads of love are present and bind us with each other and the whole of creation.

CHAPTER 94

SENDING ME SIGNS

Jocelyn

Since the squirrel sighting, there have been countless occasions when I knew Kevin was sending me signs. One that happened shortly after the squirrel involved a seagull. I was taking my son to get the latest iPhone. I hated the prospect of waiting in line at the Apple Store, but I took him anyway because there wasn't much that made him happy at that time. On the way, we drove by the house of one of our best friends. We saw her outside, so we stopped to say hello.

She told me she was thinking about what to say at Kevin's upcoming life celebration and had planned to tell the seagull story. I didn't know what story she was talking about, so she explained what she meant. Apparently, before I met Kevin, this friend and Kevin had been walking on the beach and came across a seagull that was badly injured and couldn't fly. Kevin took off his jacket and wrapped the seagull in it. They took it to a wildlife bird rescue and he paid for x-rays and surgery to heal the bird. Seagulls are a dime a dozen in Santa Barbara, but it was such a

Kevin thing to do. The bird recovered and was released back into the wild.

We left our friend's house and went directly to the Apple Store. As we were leaving the store a few hours later, there was a seagull in the parking lot. This bird was clearly badly injured and couldn't fly. Every time it tried to stand up, its neck fell to the side and it toppled over. I knew it was Kevin—it had to be. As I said, I had never heard the seagull story before, and here just a few hours later the same thing was happening before my eyes.

My son and I blocked the bird in with our car so nobody would run over it. We watched it for a while, hoping it would get up and fly. I figured it had flown into something and was just stunned. When it didn't look like it was going to get up, I called the wildlife bird rescue and got the address for where to take it. My son took his jacket off and we started to approach it. Seagulls don't look that big in the air, but on the ground in front of you, they look huge and their beaks look like they could do some serious damage. When we were a few feet from the seagull, it stood up and flew off. Again, as with the squirrel, in a later writing Kevin told me that yes, the seagull had been a sign from him to let us know he was there.

I've had many other similar experiences over the last couple of years, in many different contexts and situations. Invariably when I tell someone about the squirrel or the seagull story, they have a similar experience to share about a sign from someone they loved who has gone before them.

CHAPTER 95

A UNIVERSE OF
MULTIPLE REALITIES

Catherine

We can experience enchantment and wonder in our lives. We live in a universe of multiple realities—physical, individual, collective, and cultural. Far too frequently, we mistrust our inner voice and rely on external or traditional reference points to direct us and make sense of our world. We defer to sources outside ourselves to delineate for us what's possible or true, be they people, knowledge, history, or science. Yet we often neglect our most essential and primal sources of knowing, which are our direct experiences and ourselves.

Sadly, we sometimes hand over authority and power to other people or institutions, in the process forgetting our inner wisdom. It's our heart, our center, our spirit that contains and connects us to our greatest truth. These are gifts we each have been given in order that we might have both a biological life and an unending spiritual connection to the divine.

288

Kevin embraced the gift of life and also the gift of New Life. He lived a life that mattered. He didn't resist what life had given him, even the difficult parts like brain cancer and death. He continued to share and give of himself in states of diminished consciousness, as well as after death. It wasn't the afterlife that welcomed Kevin, but New Life. This same invitation to New Life is offered to us every moment, wherever we exist.

Like hundreds of others I've sat with, Jocelyn and Kevin allowed themselves to feel the love, grace, and connection that was always alive and well inside them. Theirs is a true story of human love, connection, heroism, and transcendence. But we each have our own unique, profound, and life-altering experiences of wonder and grace.

I encourage you to share your stories about where you have been touched, moved, and transformed. When we dare to share our truths, we expand beyond our small constructs of ourselves and others, which allows us to realize our authentic connections. In the wake of a love that's willing to express, expose, and offer itself, our fractured world begins to heal and change. Shifting our attachments from our mind-based sensors allows us to hold love-based heart and soul realities.

We don't have to wait to die to experience an expanded sense of reality or homecoming. Divine homecoming always lies within us.

CHAPTER 96

HE ISN'T GONE

Jocelyn

As I write this, it's been almost six years since Kevin died. During this time, I have had many writings with Catherine. Kevin is exactly the same as he was when he was alive. He has the same sense of humor and we still laugh together over funny things one of us will say. He still chides me over our differences. He always tells me how much he loves me and uses the same sappy terms of endearment. He encourages me when I'm feeling down or overwhelmed, and congratulates me when he thinks I'm making good decisions.

During every writing, we have in-depth discussions concerning what's happening with our children, just like we did when he was alive and we would talk over our kids' challenges and accomplishments. He knows everything that's going on with them and will make specific comments on things they are doing. For instance, he was thrilled when our youngest son decided to take up guitar, which Kevin himself loved to play. He shares my happiness when they are doing well and my disappointment when they aren't. I still feel we are parenting our kids together.

If I need some guidance on what to do in a particular situation, we talk about it, just as we did when he was alive. To me, this is one of the most important parts of the writings. Because we still communicate, I don't feel like I'm going it alone with the kids.

Kevin still never forgets a birthday, anniversary, or holiday. He sends an unsolicited message through Catherine on those special days or will come to her and tell her he wants to communicate with me, and then we'll have a writing. If there is a day that he knows is going to be particularly difficult or sad for me (like July 10, the day of his surgery, or September 7, the day he died), he often sends an unsolicited message. He encourages me not to be sad, but to instead remember all the wonderful days we had together while he was alive. Always around my birthday or a holiday, he'll do something like the squirrel incident to let me know that while he isn't here with me in the physical sense, he isn't gone.

CHAPTER 97

LONELY FOR HIM

Jocelyn

My life without Kevin is lonely. I'm not often alone, but I'm lonely for him. When he was alive, we did everything together. We worked together. And when we weren't working, we were always doing things together, with or without our kids. I know most couples wouldn't like that much togetherness, but neither of us wanted it any other way.

I do have great friends I spend time with, both new ones like Catherine and old ones I've had since grade school. I've also reconnected with people who were in my life before I met Kevin, and that's been really good for me. In some ways it's easier for me to have friendships with people who don't only associate me with Kevin. When I'm with the friends we had together, Kevin being gone is like the elephant in the room. Because of this, I've lost touch with most of the couples we socialized with. This was really my doing. We often went out with other couples to dinner or a movie, and it was a really fun aspect of our lives together. But I wasn't part of a couple anymore and just felt like a third wheel going out with them after Kevin died, so I stopped.

I have our kids, and they are doing great. Our oldest son Chris, who was struggling with addiction when Kevin died, is now a shining star, at least in his parents' eyes. We both couldn't be prouder of him. He has a steady job, a nice home, a dog he loves, and is looking forward to having a family of his own one day.

Our youngest son Will is finishing high school and is thinking about becoming a lawyer like his parents. He says he wants to wear a suit to work like his dad. I feel the most badly for him because he was only nine when Kevin first got sick and 13 when he died. I think this experience has changed him for the better, just as it did Kevin when he watched his younger brother die.

When Kevin was in the ICU, one day his oncologist came in when Will was there and asked how he was doing. Will replied, "This experience can make you bitter or better. It's going to make me better." The oncologist looked at him in amazement and asked him how old he was. When Will told him he was 13, the doctor said he couldn't believe someone so young could have such a profound outlook on the situation. He told Will that he encounters family members all the time in this same situation and had never heard anyone, regardless of their age, have that kind of understanding. While Will was far too young to lose his father, I do think that this experience has given him an understanding of humanity, empathy for others, and a maturity that most kids his age lack.

When Kevin first died, so many people told me that it would get better with time. It doesn't really get better, but you get used to it. It's like a deep cut that heals but leaves an ugly scar. While you have happy moments, you are never fundamentally happy. You can't be. Or at least, I can't be—though I'm trying. I'm hoping that one day my happy moments will turn into true happiness. I'd like that, and I know that Kevin would love it because he still loves me very much, and all you want for the people you love is for them to be happy and at peace.

CHAPTER 98

INFINITE CONNECTION, LOVE, AND SOUL

Catherine

Over my many writings with Kevin and Jocelyn, I couldn't have envisioned the gifts I would receive. Stepping into this stream of energy with them continues to transform me.

In sharing these experiences, you, like me, have been invited to wade into perhaps a larger stream of reality and truths we may not have known existed. In our humanness, many of us have longed and thirsted for deeper meaning and connection with ourselves, our souls, and God. We are this fluid love, infinitely and innately one with this life and love-giving source. Our lives and expressions are also vessels. In this way we are both the well and the bucket, fully equipped by divine design to dip into ourselves—into infinite connection, love, and soul.

At times we may hold too tight a grip on the small cup of our mind. While fabulous and essential, we must remember that the mind and intellect are limited containers that don't always hold or explain all our experiences of connection and wonder.

We need look no further than our own profound moments of transcendent love and connection that the mind can't explain but that the heart knows as truth and reality. Your moments may not be like the ones described in this book, but they are no less powerful and real to you.

In life Kevin put his heart and energy into forging a divine connection. Jocelyn told me that she had always longed for a direct experience and connection with God, but wanted it to be effortless and instantaneous. We humans know in our heart that there is a "more," and that we are integrally part of it. However, in our sophistication and complexity, we forget that the "well of our heart" is our direct conduit for connection. The mind attempts to intellectualize our experiences of the divine by asking us to further divide and separate ourselves from our experiences. We set arbitrary and linear boundaries between our consciousness, essence, and soul. Sadly, often the mind pre-conceives, prejudges, or delineates how and what we can perceive, receive, and believe.

Entering experiences with an open heart lets us welcome, feel, and receive our experiences more authentically. The truth is that we can never be separated from love or our connections in any realm.

CHAPTER 99

AHAS!

Catherine

In this story, many experiences have been recounted, as well as insights and ideas shared. In reading it, you may have experienced some "ahas" of your own. We have shared an alternative lens from which to view and understand consciousness, death, connection, and our intrinsic essence. This larger lens places you in the role of the central character, as the source and resource of divine connection in your own life.

Our lives are precious, and full of meaning and connections beyond our wildest imagination. These aspects transcend the simple imagination of the mind and take form in transforming and shaping our relationships with others, our experiences and ourselves.

Kevin was and is a messenger and embodiment of what living in accordance with one's faith, love, and connection can provide. He symbolizes and personifies the heart and soul. Throughout the writings, he remains heart-based, faith-filled, clear and wise. In contrast, Jocelyn represents more a mind-based approach—afraid, resistant, angry, and craving control. Kevin's faith allowed him to surrender, accept, and receive grace's bounty. Jocelyn distrusted, rejected, and railed against all things of faith. Long before Kevin's diagnosis of brain cancer, she judged spiritual or religious believers, with the exception of Kevin, as simple people who checked their intellect at the door and had drunk the Kool-Aid. We all have areas we judge negatively, then put our blinders on to hold our judgments in place. However in doing so, we close ourselves off from potentially powerful sources of love and connection.

Kevin and Jocelyn's journey through the writings provides us with a glimpse of the boundaries and limitations of solely relying on a mind-based approach to wisdom, support, and knowing. Kevin shared and illustrated his heart-based focus, awareness, and trust with us. Consciousness, both his and ours, isn't as finite or discrete a phenomenon as we have been taught to believe.

Our consciousness and ability to connect with and through our heart or spirit are much greater than we know. Each of us, innately and intrinsically, is imbued with this capacity for unbounded connection, love, and eternal life. Increasing our heart awareness allows us to transcend living rote and habitual lives, keeping us from squelching moments of wonder and awe. We can dive into the fullness and direct experience of our life and ourselves.

Central to all of these realizations and expansions is a loving energy, source, higher power, or God that we each are intrinsically part of.

CHAPTER 100

EPIPHANY

Jocelyn

One evening a few days before Kevin's second surgery, we were sitting together in our living room. Kevin had a glass of wine in his hand and the news was on in the background. It was a normal evening, so similar to countless others we had spent together. I had just bought a video recorder because I wanted to record all the trips we had planned for the last year of his life.

I turned it on and focused it on Kevin. We talked about the trip we had just taken to Lake Arrowhead, and he commented that we would go back in a few months when the water wasn't so cold. I asked him whether he wanted to say anything to our kids, and he said a little something that he wanted each of them to know. Then he talked about love and his faith, and how he was grateful that I had never discouraged him from his "spiritual explorations."

I laughed and said, "You and your spiritual explorations!" He got a serious look on his face and told me that one day he knew I would have more faith than he did. I seriously doubted it, but he said it with such conviction that I wondered whether he knew something I didn't.

As I mentioned earlier, the day before we drove to UCLA for his surgery, he made a "bucket list" of 20 things he wanted to do before he died. The list was mostly full of places he wanted to go and people he wanted to see. The number one item on his list wasn't a person or a place—it was "Joc's epiphany."

I used to tell him that I was waiting for my "religious epiphany," where one moment I would literally be struck down and instantaneously filled with faith and the "Holy Spirit" he so often talked about. He would tell me that I had to read and study the Bible, then that faith would come to me. I didn't want to do that. I wanted immediate and complete conversion. I guess I was just too lazy to do it the hard way. I had heard about all those people who one day pray to God to be filled with his love—then "poof," it's there. They instantly feel a spiritual connection to God, and they didn't even have to slog through the Bible to get it.

I didn't receive my religious epiphany the way I wanted, but I did ultimately have one. I realize now that if I had experienced a moment when I was literally struck down with the Holy Spirit, I wouldn't have believed it. I'm just not that kind of person. In my mind, a moment like this would mean believing in something I hadn't experienced firsthand. As I said in the beginning of this book, the only way to really know something is through a direct experience. I've had that direct experience. Now I know that it really is real—all of it.

I know that most readers will never have the direct experience I've had. I hope that doesn't stop you from believing what I now believe. There are countless times in life that you don't have to have a direct experience with something to know it's true. A lot of what we learn in life is from watching other people have an experience. When a child sees someone burn their hand from putting it on a hot stove, they learn that a stove can burn them. When you see someone almost get plowed over in the crosswalk for trying to cross the street against a red light, you know that if you do that you might become road kill. While a direct experience is definitely the most impactful way to learn something, it isn't the only way.

I'm actually amazed that God cared enough about me to give me the direct experience I needed to believe in him. Why me? I'm nothing special. More than that, I was furious at the thought of a higher power that had the ability to stop Kevin from dying but didn't. Even if there was a God, I was so pissed off at him that I wanted absolutely nothing to do with him.

In all the writings I've had with Catherine, Kevin is always encouraging me not to blame God for his death. He tells me that his death wasn't a punishment to me, even though it feels that way. I still struggle with being mad at God for Kevin dying. I don't want to feel that way, but I can't help it. The amazing thing is that I know, even though I still feel this way, that God is still there for me—as he is for everyone, whether they believe in him or not. Not only is he still there for me, but he forgives me for all my mental tantrums directed toward him. Like Kevin's love, God's love is a gift—a gift I wasn't entitled to or deserved, but that was given to me anyway.

At the beginning of this book, I told you that when you were done reading it, I wanted you to feel hopeful. To know that even if you can't see them, the people you love who have gone before you are still with you. To know also that death isn't a failure and doesn't need to be feared. But most importantly, that when you leave this earth, there is something even better for you on the other side.

GOD WRITING

CHAPTER 101

THE INTERSECTION OF HEART AND SOUL

Catherine

Thank you for joining us on the journey of this story. When finalizing the end of this book, one more unsolicited writing came, but this time not for Jocelyn. I invite you to welcome and receive a message just for you.

GOD: Welcome.

Transcend the idle limitations and give wings beyond the imagination, for inward lies the heart and soul. The intersection of heart and soul is the portal to an infinite love, freedom, and vibrant connection. In this place of abiding love, there are no stop signs or speed limits to your becoming. For indeed your consciousness moves at light and soul speed, transcending the vehicles of the brain and body. Setting your pace with a slower vibration or putting your mindset in a lower gear requires your hand to always be resting on life's emergency brakes. Not so. Not so. Not so.

The intersection of heart and soul isn't just a crosswalk to the land of living and loving out loud. It is also a bridge that crosses over the ego and the intellect's need for dominance, oppression, and ceaseless validation. The intersection of heart and soul is within, accessible from any space, place, state, or realm. The intersection of heart and soul is the nexus of becoming. The intersection of heart and soul is love's connection, not the amalgamation of a longing, and not the need to externalize the route for the realization of your always-loving nature. The intersection of heart and soul has no crossing guards, since they are unnecessary for your own entry into yourself. Behold the intersection of heart and soul, gracing you with the capacity to be trans-ego and trans-intellect. Behold the intersection of heart and soul—you are the portal of the divine reality made real. You are the conduit to all the oneness, the divine heart and soul intersection within you and your essence always. Receive yourself. Love is you.

Go with God.

In this writing God offers the intersection of heart and soul as the central theme, but it's more than an idea. It's an invitation from God to you to become aware of your own heart and soul intersection. While this writing may seem heady, it actually builds upon and amplifies many insights already shared in this book.

The intersection of heart and soul entails living with our heart and arms wide open to the whole of life and spirit. In all God writings, we are given a metaphor or concepts to clarify and raise our awareness of self-imposed limitations or beliefs. As Kevin and Jocelyn experienced, having their beliefs and understanding stretched was instrumental in growing their awareness and their ability to activate and receive the power and liberation that God offers to all of us. Yes, death will come for all of us, but it doesn't have to be feared. Nor do we have to deny the pain of losing someone we love, but can take some solace and comfort that we will be reunited with them in New Life.

While this story is about Kevin dying, Jocelyn's loss, and his New Life experiences, it's really about our innate heart and soul which are designed for greater freedom of becoming, love, connection, and spirit. However, in our humanness we can get caught and forget, falling prey to ways of limiting ourselves and our experience of our fullness of being.

"Transcend the idle limitations and give wings beyond the imagination, for inward lies the heart and soul." How many of us feel we are just idling in our lives and don't ever dare to imagine our greater becoming? We hold onto limited beliefs, self-criticisms, or fears that would keep us small. At the intersection of heart and soul, which is already embedded in us, we possess wings to fly into our grander expressions of ourselves and our lives.

If this wasn't enough, we are told there are no stop signs or speed limits where our becoming is concerned. If we allow it, our consciousness can move at light and soul speed. It is our mindset and attachment to our fears that for some of us can lead us to believe in the need to always be cautious, with our hand resting on the emergency brake, ready for the dangers that may lie ahead on the roads of our lives. The pace, gas pedal, and green lights are ours for the choosing when we place our hands on the wheel of our own life.

The intersection of heart and soul isn't offered as the only way to direct safe passage and express our love and fuller life, but as a way to rise above the potholes and pitfalls of our ego and mind. Specifically, some of us prize our mind and intellect as the forever-superior navigation and guidance system. God invites us to let the truth penetrate us that heart and soul are within and always accessible, not through the mind but in all places, states, and realms, with or even without a body.

The intersection of heart and soul is eternally about our becoming, which is our ever-present loving nature. Our loving nature isn't subject to the mind's attempts to act as a crossing guard for our endless quest for governance and validation. In addition to being the portal to our becoming, the intersection of heart and soul is the very route of entering, knowing, and embracing our deeper self. We are encouraged to enact states of "trans-ego" and "trans-intellect", which means to move through and across to the other side of our ego or intellect rather than being ruled by them. The power of mastering trans-ego and trans-intellect states assists us in releasing the mental machinations, the constrictive holdings of ourselves, and any self-sabotage. These concepts have been expounded upon in depth in other writings. Basically, when we connect and activate our intersection of heart and soul, the sticky edges of our ego or intellect move to the back seat, where they are still available to give directions, whereas our heart and soul are in the driver's seat. I know that for me, I would much rather let my heart with its connecting force of love, along with my soul which is one with God and my intuition—the most sacred parts of me—steer me into richer and more expansive experiences in my life.

"Behold, you are the portal of the divine made real." I believe we are the hands and hearts of spirit on earth. Regardless of your particular beliefs or faith, life gives each of us breath, a body, and the opportunity to express and animate love. It's this kind of connection and infinite love that the intersection of heart and soul invites us to experience for ourselves and to share with others.

I hope you will open yourself to welcome and receive this invitation that concludes: "You are the conduit to all Oneness, the divine heart and soul intersection is within you and your essence always. Receive yourself. Love is you. Go with God."

REFLECTIONS
GOD'S GOLD NUGGETS

CHAPTER 102

GOD'S GOLD NUGGETS

Catherine

When I sat down to write my portion of the conclusion of this book, I did so using the same approach I take when doing a writing—though with a laptop instead of pen and paper. I opened myself to connection, direction, and a willingness to be of service. I dipped into that ever-present stream of consciousness and connection. Both Jocelyn and I have been amazed that this book seemed to write itself. Yes, a fair portion of the book was directly taken from the writings that occurred more than six years ago. The Kevin writing sessions spanned three and a half months, in various settings and circumstances. However, when I looked back at the singular God introductions taken together, there is a consistent thread among them. These introductions contain many gold nuggets to take away from the experiences, meaning, and implications of the story we have shared. The true gold lies within us. We can pan for it every day within this current of love, connection, and soul that moves within and is us.

You have journeyed down a river of experiences and insights with Jocelyn, Kevin, and me. My goal has been to help you navigate these waters whose depths you may not previously have appreciated or known. Now I invite you to briefly return with me to the landmarks embedded in the writing introductions and see, as I have, what was always hidden in plain sight—to behold some of the gold.

CHAPTER 103

THE SOUL INTUITS INNATELY

Catherine

"But the eye need not be open to see what the soul intuits innately."

"The foggy mists surround the consciousness, but the soul knows it isn't the outer focus but the inner knowing that counts."

"The windows, though foggy, can't eclipse what the soul knows, speaks and directs innately."

"The process of drawing inward does not connote vacancy, but a more soulful inhabitation."

If we look at this sharing from the perspective of a heart-based instead of a mind-based lens, it offers us new levels of understanding. We have a tendency to use the "mind's eye" and "outer focus" to direct and inform us about what we see, experience, and know. But even with all our foggy tendencies to think and overthink, there is a clarity and truth in soul that can't be eclipsed.

We are reminded that we are and always will be directly connected to this divine source. Our highest authority isn't someone or something exterior to us. No, our soul is the greatest source of our own internal wisdom and divine connection. If the word "soul" still seems too amorphous to understand, simply substitute the word "heart," "spirit," or "love." Choose the word that resonates and gives you the deepest meaning and understanding. Pause and let yourself drink in each statement, and notice not what you "think" but what you "feel or intuit innately" within your heart. This is an opportunity for you to expand from a mental conceptualization to a heart resonance and connection.

CHAPTER 104

THE HEART KNOWS NO SUCH DIVISIONS

Catherine

"The division is transparent, for the heart knows no such divisions."

"… the grace of God does shine forward …"

"The vacancy isn't a reflection of the spirit, which is full of light and vitality."

Once again, we are reminded that the heart is our conduit. While the mind may dissect and compartmentalize our experiences, the heart knows no such divisions. Grace is always available to provide us with qualities of illumination that cannot go dark. Indeed, our thoughts may tend toward negativity, darkly projecting and shading our experiences with our fear.

Going deeper into our heart space doesn't mean we are vacant. Again and again throughout all the writings, we don't see Kevin shrinking or disappearing. To the contrary, we see a man whose spirit grows in love, faith, and wisdom. We are blessed to be on this odyssey of his becoming. We must never lose sight of the fact that each one of us is lovingly given the opportunity to embrace our spirit, full of light and vitality. There is no exclusivity, nor is death the only entry point to embrace these kinds of experiences or realizations.

CHAPTER 105

THE SPIRIT OF LOVE TRANSCENDS

Catherine

"There is in this a vine of love in your family that can't be broken."

"In death's pruning, there is nothing it can take from us, for life has more to give beyond the grave."

"The spirit of love transcends the apparent separation, for in truth it is the place that has no separation."

"The heart that loves knows no boundary, for life has no barriers."

Let this wisdom wash over you. How does this speak within you about your experience and capacity to love and be loved?

Our love is eternal. We are eternal. We are the vines of love and connection to each other and to the divine that death cannot sever. The spirit of love, like the spirit within each of us, cannot be separated.

We are all part of one infinite boundary-less love. Each of us—in our individual life and expression—has been given this amazing energy, power, and connectedness called love that we all too often hide or run from. We erect barriers of fear, protectiveness, or erroneous beliefs of unworthiness. We separate ourselves from knowing and fully receiving this very divine gift, which is this: "We are love." We quest or long for it, yet we may tend to push away or downplay those peak moments when we are actually receiving and experiencing them.

We are love and we are loved. Love is our intrinsic and true nature. Love is the infinite energy that holds all realities together. Love isn't about separation. Love transcends any false places of separation within us, between us, or in our divine connection. Receive the love that is you. Dive into your own self-embrace, receptivity, and reception of this infinite love that you already are and can never be separated from.

CHAPTER 106

THE COMPASS OF LOVE

Catherine

"Turn within to the roadmap of the heart, which has etched into it each moment with great exuberance a life well lived."

"For within the journey, the compass of love has always guided the way."

"Allow True North to direct you. Your center, your union, your relationship changed—yes. But the journey isn't finished."

"Soul-to-soul, heart-to-heart, love-to-love, it is eternal and infinite."

Our attention is called to our heart and our soul as infinite sources of love. Soul, heart, and love are not mere abstract ideas or concepts. They are essential tools to guide, actively engage, and live our lives fully. Nothing is said here about the guidance system of our mind or intellect. We are invited to turn to the roadmap of our hearts, and we are reminded to recall and have reverence for the exuberant moments of our lives well lived. It's not simply the good moments, the superior or achieving moments, but "each moment in all exuberance."

This represents such an empowering and profound possibility, particularly once these moments have been etched in our heart, becoming a realization and reality. How might the world be different if we didn't let our smallness, perceived limitations, and fear direct us? What would our lives, individually and collectively, be like if we truly let "the compass of love" guide us?

Each moment in which we choose to love and create is a moment well lived. The reassurance being offered here is that our journey is never over. Here, the divine's invitation to each of us is to live this eternal and infinite journey we have been given:

"Soul-to-soul, heart-to-heart, love-to-love ...."

CHAPTER 107

YOUR SPIRIT, YOUR HEART IS...

Catherine

"This is necessary to know that you are more than these tentacles that service everyone and everything. These are attached to a center that contains not only the massive brain but a sensing, loving center that is not limited by all these boundaries of demands, problems, realities, and life factors."

"You are not such a developed being that you have forgotten your center."

"... know it's okay to be held, to let yourself be held."

"Water is all about you in support, in that you can never actually sink."

"For you are your center."

"Your spirit, your heart IS ..."

Our complex brain and thought centers are sometimes contrasted with our heart and spirit centers. This highlights an important way we can become free from our mind's holding of demands, problems, realities, or life factors.

Not only do we forget our heart and soul as conduits of love and support, we may also push away or reject others' attempts to lovingly care and support us. Is it any wonder we find ourselves exhausted from directing our energy toward others, and also exerting energy trying to hold others at bay from caring for us? While we tell ourselves it's okay, even preferable to help and hold another, we resist and reject letting ourselves be helped or held. Yet the supporting waters of fluid love and the divine are always about us.

Though at times we live our lives as if we are constantly drowning, we can never really sink, "For you, you are your center." You are not all the things your mind, society, and social comparisons tell you. You are not your possessions. You are not your achievements. You are not your income. More importantly, you are not your ego or your needs. You are not the things you use to judge or critique yourself or others. We all know how life feels when we live from these kinds of ego and scarcity-based fears and criticisms.

Allow yourself to fully exhale and breathe in this truth. "Your spirit, your heart IS ..." What if each day we could begin from this realization? The truth of our center, our spirit, and our heart is that we are far more infinite, wise, divine, and loving than we have ever dared to imagine.

CHAPTER 108

THE THIRST FOR A DEEPER CONNECTION

Catherine

"So the 'hows' and 'whats' that the mind requests and even demands punctuation for aren't the language of the heart and soul. For the mind says, 'I must see it to experience it. I must collapse my experiences into segmented and discriminate realities for the purpose of my linear nature.' The heart and soul hold no such artificial or contrived boundaries. Though it appears to the physical eye that something has ended, to the heart and soul it isn't so. For love is unending and eternal, as is soul—connection vowed and sealed so deep within that it does not end with a physical passage or ending. No, the love in its fluid nature pours itself forth without the need for a vessel or a bodily cup to contain or express it. For love is greater than all these languages that the mind engages."

Allow yourself to feel the enormity of what is being offered here. Don't receive this wisdom from the mind that uses its tactics of bait and switch to keep us from the deeper truths of our heart and soul. We who thirst for a deeper connection within ourselves, with each other and the divine, are being asked to know our own true nature and essence. "For love is unending and eternal as is soul." The mind has languages, and by their very existence they define how and what we see and conceive of. This abstract concept called love is very real, powerful, and ever-present in and as us.

"Love is unlimited. It is birthed within and it has no end. It is eternal, as you are. Allow the warmth of love, that light between you and the beloved, to cradle you in arms that now seem formless but are more expansive and stronger than they have ever been."

We need look no further than our own heart to welcome, receive, and express this love. The "beloved" in this case isn't just a person, but the divine beloved, a loving presence and energy that though formless illuminates and holds us, the nexus of eternal love within.

CHAPTER 109

NEW LIFE

Catherine

"Happy is a fragment, a filament of light in memory that is dancing on the shadow of loss and missing. But warm yourself to that light of love, that though the period has appeared in the physical, it still burns bright. Not an ember, but a brilliant lighthouse saying, 'In this place of our deep love and joining, I am guiding, loving, ever present, steering you to me by the light of this love we share.' This love that two know can be as the divine extension of self, of soul, of connection, of union, knows not the silence nor the distance."

What a relief it is that we are always one with and in this divine connection. We are urged to release our allegiance to linear constructs of separation and endings. The divine not only bestows upon us precious gifts to experience life, but also continues those offerings upon our physical death with New Life.

"It is the heart that crosses a seeming divide that separates the realities of life and 'New Life'."

"New Life celebrates all. New Life knows that blood is only necessary in the body, that breath is only necessary in the body."

"But love—love stands as the very essence of all creation in all realms, life or New Life."

"Life is love, and love is life—and this cannot be severed, no matter."

How many of us fear death? How many wonder and worry about these unknowable and unreachable realities our mind cannot define? This is the fodder that existential crises are made of. Yet God is saying our love and essence become New Life. Concerning our fears about death, God says:

"This is God's way. Not the vocabulary of endings, not the punctuation of loss and longing, not the punishment or forgetting, but the way of divine union. Your innate capacity is to join in divine love, which a physical body has no power to dictate over. Divine love, birthed between you and the beloved, brings heaven and form to earth in full expression."

The central message in all the writings is that we are love, soul, and divine connection. Love is our essence and never can be extinguished. We are created and given free will to live this love, both in our physical life and in the New Life that awaits us.

The final words of the divine in this last writing are eloquent, simple and direct.

"Love has no period. Union has no end. Life to New Life, you and the beloved eternally connected in heart and soul. This is the gift that has no end!"

CHAPTER 110

THE BUCKET LIST

Catherine

Jocelyn has exposed and shared her own story of struggle, loss, grief and eternal love. Her life was never the same after Kevin's brain cancer diagnosis in 2009. Regardless of the difficulties and tragedies she endured, love and God had more life to unfold for her.

Kevin created a "bucket list" of what he wanted to accomplish in the remainder of his life. Sadly, the majority of these items were never realized. The number one item on his list was "Joc's epiphany." Jocelyn told me she had longed for an experience of the Holy Spirit her whole life. Never having one only served to further anger and separate her from God.

Unknowingly prophetic, Kevin told her that same evening more than six years ago that he trusted she would one day have more faith than he did. From her perspective, not only could there be no God, but if there was one, then why did he purposely inflict pain and suffering?

Throughout all the writings, Kevin encourages Jocelyn to have faith. He tells her death is not a failure and not to blame

324

God. With the "Need Help—Call Jesus, 1 (555) I GOT GOD" and "Jesus is pulling for you" experiences, Kevin calls Jocelyn's attention to spiritual realms. However, watching her husband—a faithful, loving, kind, and good person—suffer and die only created and fueled for her more hopelessness, despair, anger, and bitterness. Jocelyn having faith of any sort, not to mention faith greater than Kevin's, wasn't just improbable, it seemed downright impossible.

Grace appears in our lives in the most unsuspecting and unanticipated ways. The irony is that through the writings with Kevin and God, Jocelyn actually received the epiphany she had awaited and longed for her whole life. What a selfless act on Kevin's behalf to have made Jocelyn's epiphany his number one bucket list item.

The second item on Kevin's list was "visit Israel and the Holy Land." Although he never physically took that journey, I believe he reached the Holy Land. He arrived safe and sound, and he continues to send back messages to Jocelyn and all of us in the writings. Jocelyn and I could not have imagined that we would collaborate and write this book.

This brings me to the third item on Kevin's bucket list, which was "To Take a Missions Trip" and serve others. I believe that in our sharing of Kevin and his story, this has been accomplished as well. His story, the man he was and still is in spirit, continues his mission to be of service to others.

Who could have imagined that the top three items of importance to Kevin would come to fruition? Amazingly they did, in ways that could never have been thought possible. Yet they represent miracles of sorts, very powerful, true and real.

What's on your bucket list? What love, heart, and soul connections do you long for in your life? Perhaps the message is we shouldn't wait to realize and experience them. We don't need all the external realities to line up in our favor to experience these kinds of loving heart and soul connections. We only need to remind ourselves to dip that bucket into our own hearts and the stream of divine and loving connection, allowing ourselves to experience everything, and be filled.

Expanding our minds, accessing our hearts, and connecting with our inner divinity and wisdom allow us to behold and receive wonder in our every day, extraordinary lives. Welcome, open, and trust yourself, your heart, and your own experiences of grace and love.

* * *

ACKNOWLEDGMENTS

Catherine A. Weissenberg

My deepest, soul-filled gratitude goes to God, the source of everything in the universe. Through this process I've been stretched—kicking and screaming at times—but always stepping into greater wonder and faith. Making my gift public through this book comes with some fear, but God always soothes my heart and gives me strength to live boldly. I do my best to do the will of God.

My heartfelt thanks go to everyone who held, rocked and supported our "book baby." This book has been a community effort; I am forever grateful for the tending, support, and generosity of time and spirit from all those who have ushered this project along.

Of course, a special thanks to my co-conceiver, Jocelyn, who said, "If you want to write this story, I'll help you." We have been in a long but fruitful labor to deliver this book. Witnessing Jocelyn's transformation—emotionally, spiritually and personally—was and is inspiring. I commend her willingness to transcend her pain and be propelled by her love for

Kevin to share this story. Being vulnerable is difficult. This book would never have been drafted without Jocelyn pouring herself out and conquering her reluctance and fears. She is a fighter, and we had several mudwrestling events along the way. We disagreed, we laughed, we cried, we challenged each other. Our stylistic differences are representative of our personalities, yet our shared goal bonded us together and made us love one another despite them. Kevin is Jocelyn's most precious treasure, and I am eternally grateful that she shared him with me and our readers. Writing this book and Kevin's ongoing presence and support, have helped to lighten Jocelyn's grief and move forward with her life.

A gigantic thank you goes to Kevin. He was generous in sharing his love and wisdom, demonstrating for all of us that it's never too late to realize one's mission.

Boundless gratitude also goes to my husband. Without his love, patience, support and timely encouragement, there would not be a book. Throughout our 29 years together, he has always known when to speak out and when to let me struggle. He gently reminds me to trust my own wings.

For their emotional support and willingness to talk in detail about aspects of this project, special thanks to my dear friends, Virginia and Terri.

I believe God places particular intersections of abilities, people, and situations into our lives. Most of the time we can't see the pattern, the opportunities and gifts. Only in hindsight is the perfect alignment revealed. Creating this book is just such an experience. I acknowledge and thank in advance our readers for gifts which they will bring to us.

Many, many folks have offered edits, insights and feedback to refine our telling of this story. My thanks go first to Vicky Garske, my dear friend for some 20 years. She followed her "knowing" by recommending that Jocelyn have that first writing with me. Vicky was present in the beginning of this story and shared her tap-my-finger experience with Kevin. She also contributed her talents to the proofing process. Words cannot convey my gratitude to Robin Lynn-Jacobs who proofed our manuscript to the point of exhaustion. She was a master mid-wife in helping us birth this book. Robin encouraged me to be patient, remember to breathe and appreciate that this project has its own timing and destiny. Gratitude and hugs also go to Gina Lane, who expertly edited multiple versions of this manuscript (and also typed thousands of pages of writings over the years).

Praise to our book editor, David Ord, whose fine touch improved the telling of this story. His polishing expertise and technique were invaluable. Thank you to Dr. Gary Schwartz for writing the Foreword for this book. We are grateful that a seasoned expert in the field of advanced consciousness such as Dr. Schwartz recognizes and legitimizes the power of this type of work. Gratitude to Johanna Maaghul, our agent. She saw the value of this book and believed in it from the beginning. She was able to secure a publishing company for us, although ultimately we decided to put our "book baby" in our own customized carriage.

With arms wide open, thanks to all of you who took this story into your hearts. Our beta readers are too many to name individually. Trust that your handprints and loving support are in this book. Thanks to IANDS Santa Barbara and Word and Life of Santa Barbara who invited us to present our story to their audiences. As authors, Jocelyn and I were inspired by the enthusiasm flowing from all the aforementioned friends, colleagues, and audiences.

Lastly, I acknowledge my profound gratitude for this gift, which allows me to be part of the journey into the intimate places of soul, spirit and love.

Jocelyn Montanaro

Here is the part where I get to thank some people that I cherish, or drove nuts in the process of writing this book. Some folks for even longer than that!

To Catherine Weissenberg, my co-author. There was nobody I drove nuts more than Catherine. During this process we laughed so hard for so many hours that our sides ached. We also both cried at times during the long and arduous editing process. This book meant so much to Catherine and me that we wanted it to be perfect. As we are both imperfect beings (and I'll admit that my imperfections may exceed hers) we drove each other a bit crazy getting the "baby," as we called our book, born. Throughout it all, I was beyond grateful and blessed by her wonderful gift, which made the impossible, possible. But Catherine's friendship was, and still is, just as wonderful a gift to me. I made a lifelong bestie, at a time in my life when I really needed one. A perfect example of divine intervention!

To Rob Saperstein, Catherine's husband. I think that poor man felt like he had stepped into the Twilight Zone sometimes with me and Catherine. For years, I was a constant presence in their lives, both in and out of their home. During it all Rob was funny and gracious and often the calming presence Catherine and I needed. Rob played an integral part in writing this book. He read it as we went along, and his feelings and feedback about the content helped to shape how I told the story. I can't thank Rob enough for all he did for both Catherine and me, but more importantly for his friendship. It means the world to me.

To Victoria and Susan Lindenauer, who have been friends of Kevin and mine for decades. Vicki was the maid of honor at our wedding and she was there for the birth of our first child. Sue was my vacation buddy who kept me sane during Kevin's illness with those well-timed Cabo trips. Both of them helped with my youngest son during Kevin's illness and hospitalization. When I have conversations with myself in my head, it is Vicki and Sue I talk things over with. They are so much more than friends, and this acknowledgment doesn't in any way begin to cover what they mean to me.

To Blythe Coulter, who is my sister in all ways except DNA. When everything went south after Kevin's surgery, she made the four-hour drive in the middle of the night to be with me and the kids. She stayed and helped me navigate all the life and death decisions that had to be made during those early days when I couldn't think straight. Luckily, she is brilliant and was able to do that with ease and a calm focus that I didn't have but desperately needed. Blythe is a rock, and I've relied on her more times than I can count over the last 30 years.

To the Phreaners, our next door neighbors and great friends. We spent many vacations together when our kids were younger, either at Mammoth in the winter or Bass Lake in the summer. Kevin would often wander over to their house after work with a bottle of wine to share. When Kevin was in the hospital, they took in our Shih Tzu, Sophie. When we finally came home, Sophie wanted to stay with the Phreaners. But that is how they are. Everyone wants to be a Phreaner because their home is happy and filled with love and support.

To Jim Slater, one of Kevin's best friends and his business partner. His wife Marian is the sweetest and most loving woman I've ever met. Their friendship and support for all these years, even now, gives me a connection to Kevin that I cherish.

To Monte Fraker, who I've known since the 3rd grade, when we used to eat craft paste together! His laughter, friendship, and unwavering faith in God were a big comfort to me during that time and still to this day.

A special shout out to my friend Lynn Dodge. I told Lynn this story right after meeting her for the first time at an organized dog walk. Contrary to my concern that she would think I was nuts, she was immediately interested in the story, even fascinated. Lynn gave me the courage to write the first words.

To Theresa Cordero (the world's number one Patriots fan) one of my dearest friends. Theresa read an early draft and loved it so much that she connected Catherine and me with people in the publishing world who helped us get the ball rolling. You're the bomb, Tree!

To Robin Lynn-Jacobs—editor supreme. I had never met Robin before I started this project with Catherine. From the first draft until the finished product, Robin combed over every word and analyzed all the punctuation. Every time Robin proofed the book, she caught things that everyone else (even paid professionals) missed. She never refused a request for help, even though all she got out of it was our gratitude. The most amazing part of it all was that she did it with the calmest of demeanors, something Catherine and I lacked at times during the arduous editing process. All I can say is thank you Robin, from the bottom of my heart. We owe you big time.

To Gina Lane, one of the smartest and funniest women I know. A brilliant writer, a fabulous editor, and an even better friend. Gina has spent more time than anyone other than Catherine, Robin and me editing our book. It wouldn't be the polished manuscript it became without her help. Love you, girlfriend!

To Olivia Villalovos, my young, beautiful and wise-beyond-her-years friend. Your support, encouragement and friendship have been an unexpected blessing in my life.

To Jennifer Huebner, the little sister I never had as a kid but got as an adult. You are an undyingly loyal and cherished friend. You always think the best of everyone, and you live your life with a kindness that reminds me of Kevin.

Finally, to my sister Victoria Garske, to whom I dedicated the book. I have to say a few more words about all the help she has given me from the time Kevin first got sick. When we were in

Hawaii and Kevin was first diagnosed with brain cancer, I called Vicky before anyone else, and she was the first person waiting for me at the airport to take Kevin home. During his final surgery, she shuttled my youngest son back and forth to UCLA and stayed as needed. She drove Catherine from Santa Barbara to UCLA to do the pivotal writing that changed my plans for Kevin. During the long editing process of the book, she stepped in for me when I couldn't look at the manuscript one more time. There wouldn't be a book without Vicky, and for that I owe her my unending gratitude.

To all the early readers whose feedback helped us shape this book. Each and every one of you made an invaluable contribution.

To my children who watched me drop everything else in my life but this book for quite a long time. Thanks, you guys, for gutting it out with me!

ABOUT THE AUTHORS

CATHERINE A. WEISSENBERG

For several decades, Catherine Weissenberg has been sharing her unique ability to communicate and dialogue with God, the deceased, and coma patients. To retain a lasting record of these communications, Catherine writes the dialogues longhand as they occur, and calls them "Writings." In actuality, she connects with the stream of universal consciousness and transforms that energy into prose. When asked to explain her gift, Catherine states, "I believe God and those we love are always in our midst. There is a God, a consciousness, a stream of love that runs within all of us. I'm able to connect and transform this flow into words which all of us can understand. This energy – I like to refer to it as a 'Love Stream' – is ever-present for everyone. I offer my work to facilitate that connection."

Although the Writings are specific to the recipient or group, they are beautiful in imagery and metaphor, often touching upon the universal themes of self-growth, interpersonal relationships and life challenges. In addition to publishing *Beyond Ever After: A Heart-to-Heart Journey Through Death and the Afterlife,* Catherine has created Loveality,® a love-based reality, to bring the wisdom and transformative energy of the Writings to a broader audience. For more information about Loveality, please visit her website at Loveality.net.

A Communication facilitator and consultant, Catherine holds a Master of Arts degree in Communication. She also facilitates group retreats, which sometimes include Writings. She has taught college level communication and served in leadership roles in nonprofit and volunteer organizations. Catherine is a mother and wife, and lives in California.

JOCELYN MONTANARO

Jocelyn Montanaro considers herself a reluctant messenger. She loved her relatively traditional life as a wife, mother and part-time lawyer. She would not have traded places with anyone. There were only two areas that Jocelyn didn't share with Kevin, her husband: a belief in God and an active involvement in organized religion. That Jocelyn would write a book about accepting God's love and communicating with the dead was about as likely as her being elected pope.

Educated on the East Coast and in Europe, Jocelyn has both a law degree and a bachelor's in International Studies. She also studied International Business and Social Etiquette at the Institut Villa Pierrefeu in Switzerland. She lives in Southern California.

LET THE JOURNEY CONTINUE

www.beyondeverafter.com

We don't want this amazing journey to end!

We would love to stay in touch and hear about your own Beyond Ever After stories and experiences.

Please visit our website at www.beyondeverafter.com where you can contact us, learn about our upcoming events, view our blog, and share your own experiences.

You can also follow us on Facebook at Beyond Ever After.

Beyond
Ever After

Made in USA - Kendallville, IN
1049272_9781733172738
02.11.2020 0813